Seasons, Sacraments and Sacramentals

Dennis C. Smolarski, SJ

LITURGY
TRAINING
PUBLICATIONS

Acknowledgments

The essays in this book first appeared in various issues of the magazine *Rite* (which, prior to the year 2000, was named *Liturgy 90*) between the years 1995 and 2003. All of the essays have been revised according to the 2002 edition of the *General Instruction of the Roman Missal* and other recent Vatican documents. The author, Dennis C. Smolarski, SJ, continues to write the Q&A column in *Rite* magazine. To subscribe, go to www.ltp.org or call 1-800-933-4213.

Q&A: SEASONS, SACRAMENTS AND SACRAMENTALS ©2003 Archdiocese of Chicago: Liturgy Training Publications, 1800 North Hermitage Avenue, Chicago IL 60622-1101; 1-800-933-1800, fax 1-800-933-7094, e-mail orders@ltp.org. All rights reserved. See our website at www.ltp.org.

This book was edited by David Philippart, with assistance from Betsy Anders. The initial design is by Anna Manhart, final design by Larry Cope. The production editor was Kris Fankhouser and the typesetting was done by Mark Hollopeter in Esprit and Officina. The cover and interior art is a modification by Larry Cope of the original Q&A logo designed by Luba Lukova.

Printed in the United States of America.

Library of Congress Control Number: 2002115620

ISBN 1-56854-391-3

QASEA

Table of Contents

The Seasons

Baptism and Confirmation

Marriage

Penance

The Seasons

What are the guidelines or restrictions concerning celebrating weddings or baptisms during Advent or Lent?

Let me first address the issue of marriages and then reflect on baptisms. Many older Catholics may remember that prior to the Second Vatican Council there were restrictions about weddings during Advent and Lent. Although Catholics were discouraged from marrying during these seasons, weddings in themselves were not forbidden. Only the celebration of the nuptial blessing and the nuptial Mass were; the rite of marriage outside of Mass could be used. What was frowned upon was a degree of festivity that seemed incompatible with the somberness of these two liturgical seasons. Because of these restrictions, in many places few, if any, weddings took place in churches during Advent and Lent. If a wedding did occur, it usually took place in a parlor of the rectory, as did most "mixed marriages" between a Catholic and a non-Catholic.

Vatican II's *Constitution on the Sacred Liturgy* (CSL) decreed that the nuptial blessing should always be given at the marriage of Catholics (78), thus removing the former restriction. But the revised marriage rite issued in 1969 continued to advise that the couple contemplating marriage should respect the character of the days of Advent, Lent and other days of penance, for example, November 2 (All Souls Day) (see the 1969 Introduction of the *Rite of Marriage,* 11, and the 1990 Introduction, 32). In addition, the Vatican's 1988 *Circular Letter Concerning the Preparation and Celebration of the Easter Feasts* (CL) promulgated a new restriction: It specifically forbade the celebration of marriage on Good Friday and Holy Saturday (61, 75), a prohibition that has now been included in the revised 1990 Introduction of the *Rite of Marriage* (32).

Although canonical and liturgical laws do not expressly forbid the celebration of weddings during Advent and Lent, there is the specific counsel that the bridal couple should "respect" the nature and character of the seasons. This suggests several things.

Perhaps a first step is to review the current practices and see how well people do, in fact, "respect" Advent and Lent: Are there are any major differences between how weddings are celebrated in Advent, Lent and at other times?

Next, "respecting" the nature of Advent and Lent should at least mean that the couple is informed that such seasons, as seasons of preparation, reflection and (in the case of Lent) penance, are inappropriate times for the festivity usually associated with weddings. Thus, perhaps, the couple should consider other times of the year.

If compelling reasons exist for scheduling a wedding during Advent or Lent (and perhaps what is truly a "compelling" reason should be predetermined so that people don't plead for discount airfares or off-season hotel rates as "compelling reasons"), the parish needs to address how the wedding celebration should remain consistent with the liturgical mood that the parish wishes to achieve during Advent or Lent. One cannot pretend during a wedding that it is temporarily not Advent or Lent and completely ignore the ambience of the community's liturgical life. One cannot allow florists to remove purple bunting or other elements of the seasonal environment simply because they clash with elaborate floral displays.

In particular, all should recall that there are general prohibitions on the use of flowers and instrumental music during Advent and Lent. Exceptions are permitted for major feasts, but not for weddings. (See 2002 *General Instruction of the Roman Missal* [GIRM], 305, and paragraph 236 of the *Ceremonial of Bishops* [CB] for Advent and paragraph 252 for Lent. Concerning Advent, the CB speaks about "moderation" in music and floral decorations.)

If Advent and Lent mean anything to the local community, then wedding celebrations during those seasons should be devoid of flowers (perhaps including bridal bouquets!) and of instrumental music.

Perhaps the nature of the seasons should also apply to the number of attendants involved. Numerous bridesmaids and groomsmen would also seem to be inconsistent with the somberness and simplicity of these liturgical seasons. So if weddings do take place during Advent and Lent, perhaps the attendants should be limited to the required two witnesses alone.

A careful examination of the current liturgical laws show them to be flexible in providing a couple with the opportunity for the church's special nuptial blessing whenever they celebrate their marriage, even during Advent or Lent, but also suggest that weddings must respect the rhythm of the liturgical year. It is a challenge for every parish staff to help guide couples planning marriage to celebrate the occasion with proper festivity, yet be conscious that every celebration, including a wedding, must respect the more important dynamics of the church's liturgical year.

Now, what about baptisms? The spirit of the *Rite of Christian Initiation of Adults* (RCIA) suggests that, normally, *adult* baptisms be celebrated once a year, at the Easter Vigil. So the question is whether it is permitted to celebrate the baptism of *infants* during Lent. (The contemporary understanding of Advent contains little association with preparation for baptism, so there is no urgent reason to avoid celebrating baptism during Advent, except that perhaps celebrating baptism in early January would unite infant baptisms to the feast of Christ's own baptism.)

The CL forbids the celebration of baptism and confirmation on Good Friday and Holy Saturday. In fact, it also states that baptism and confirmation should not be celebrated any day of Holy Week (27).

Though not explicitly stated, the logic behind the rule is clear. Since all of Lent is a preparation for the celebration of Christian initiation through baptism, confirmation and eucharist at the Easter Vigil, one should not anticipate what properly belongs at the Vigil that begins the 50-day celebration of Easter.

Although the earlier days of Lent are not explicitly mentioned in the CL, since they too are specially associated with baptismal preparation, especially with the public rites of the RCIA, many would argue that it is also inconsistent to celebrate any baptisms (or confirmations) at any time during this special period before Easter, thereby inappropriately juxtaposing the preparation rites with those of initiation, even if it is the initiation of infants or the confirming of older children or adolescents.

The vision of the RCIA is that adults (and children of catechetical age) are to be baptized and confirmed at the Easter Vigil, and not earlier. Logic and consistency would recommend a similar parish policy for the baptism of infants and the confirmation of children already baptized as infants. The ideal policy would be for parishes not to schedule any infant baptisms during Lent and delay all of them until the Easter Vigil or any given Sunday of the Easter season. Of course, emergency baptisms for newborns can never be planned and should always be accommodated. But when planning is possible, parish communities should respect the rhythm and the ancient meaning of Lent and not compromise the period of baptismal preparation by anticipating the celebration of baptism for minor reasons.

Where is the best place during the liturgy to bless the Advent wreath for the First Sunday of Advent? Additionally, for the following Sundays, when should we do the lighting? Do we need to have a wreath in the daily Mass chapel? Once the wreath is blessed at one Mass, do you need to bless it at every weekend liturgy? What about the Christmas blessing of the Nativity scene? Do you bless the Nativity scene at every Mass or only once?

Devotional items such as the Advent wreath or the Christmas crèche are not an integral part of the Roman rite, in contrast to the ashes blessed and imposed on Ash Wednesday, the palms blessed on Palm Sunday, the holy oils blessed at the Chrism Mass or the Easter candle lit at the Easter Vigil. Because they are items associated with popular devotions, rather than objects with liturgical significance, neither wreath nor crèche needs to be placed in a church or chapel. In addition, care should be taken about whether and how any sort of acknowledgment of any such non-liturgical (yet often very devotional) item is integrated into the Roman liturgy. We always need to be careful about highlighting secondary, albeit popular, devotional items, lest they be given more prominence than they deserve and perhaps overshadow the more fundamental symbols of the Roman liturgical tradition.

Prior to the Second Vatican Council, the Advent wreath was primarily a domestic devotion. Families were encouraged to create an Advent wreath in their homes in a prominent location, but it was rare to find such a wreath in church. After the Council, but before the revised *Book of Blessings* (BB) appeared, it became increasingly popular to set up a wreath in churches and even smaller chapels, and various unofficial ceremonies for blessing the wreath appeared in print. Some of these rites suggested that the blessing and lighting of the Advent wreath take place as part of the opening rites. This seems to have been modeled after the blessing of the fire and lighting of the Easter candle at the beginning of the Easter Vigil or the ancient *lucenarium* (candle lighting) service sometimes included at the beginning of Evening Prayer.

When the U.S. edition of the revised BB was published in 1989, it included an "Order for the Blessing of an Advent Wreath" during Mass (Chapter 47, 1509). This order follows the standard format for any blessing, that is, a prayer of blessing follows a liturgy of the word and intercessory prayers. After the prayer of blessing, the person or object just blessed is acknowledged in some way. For example, a scapular is handed to the one who will wear it, those receiving rosaries are supposed to say at least part of the rosary and so forth. Thus the official U.S. rite places the blessing of the Advent wreath at the conclusion of the liturgy of the word, with the prayer of blessing constituting the concluding prayer of the general intercessions. After the blessing, the first candle is lit.

The BB is very reserved about the use and placement of the Advent wreath. Traditionally, the wreath is suspended from the ceiling, and the BB notes this location first (1512). In such a location, it would not be easy to light the candles during the liturgy. The BB then notes that if the wreath is located in the sanctuary, it should not obscure the primary liturgical focal points of chair, ambo and altar, nor should it interfere with the liturgical action.

The BB also advises (1513) that after the First Sunday of Advent, the appropriate number of candles of the wreath may be lit before Mass (as is done with the Easter candle after the Vigil). It is permitted, however, to light the candles of the wreath without any additional text immediately before the opening prayer.

The BB offers no particular guidance about repeating the blessing and lighting of the wreath on the First Sunday of Advent, in contrast to what is done on Ash Wednesday and Palm Sunday. The blessing of palms and ashes may be repeated, but these rites include alternative texts that explicitly invoke God's blessing on the people assembled. The rites for blessing palms and ashes focus on items that are taken by the faithful out of the church. In contrast, the Advent wreath is a seasonal object (like the Easter candle) that remains part of the worship environment. Thus it seems appropriate to bless the wreath once, at the first Mass of the First Sunday of Advent. If it is pastorally appropriate to call attention to the wreath at other Masses, it would seem better to light it in a simple way immediately before the opening prayer rather than "re-bless" an object already blessed.

I would also suggest a similar restraint in acknowledging the Christmas crèche. In fact, the BB notes that the manger must *not* be set up in the sanctuary (1544). Rather than include a formal blessing of the crèche, some parishes acknowledge its devotional importance by placing the figure of the infant Jesus in the crib at the beginning of Midnight Mass while the opening song is sung and then solemnly incensing the crèche as part of the initial incensation of the Mass. Highlighting the historical events of Bethlehem, though necessary for our faith, can distract from the importance of welcoming Christ's continued "advent" into our world in the present and our "waiting in joyful hope for the coming of our Savior" in his glory.

The *Constitution on the Sacred Liturgy* gave us wise counsel when it reminded us that devotions are always secondary to the liturgy, which surpasses any devotion (13). Even though devotions such as the Advent wreath and the Christmas crèche are related to an important liturgical season, they are still popular devotions; care should always be taken that they not be accorded an exaggerated importance. Of course, they can be incorporated into the ambience of the season to help us focus on the person of the Christ who is with us "always, until the end of time" (Matthew 28:20).

What readings do we use at the 4:30 PM Christmas Eve Mass? The vigil readings are not what the parents of the children attending want to hear!

The practice of "anticipating" the celebration of Sunday or a holy day by attending Mass the preceding evening has become more and more widespread after the promulgation of the 1983 Code of Canon Law, which gave general permission to this practice (1248, section 1). Between 1967, when this practice was first mentioned in the *Eucharisticum mysterium,* and 1983, permission to schedule such "anticipated" Masses varied from country to country and diocese to diocese. Typically, the liturgical readings used for a Vigil Mass are those prescribed for the Sunday itself, but there are several solemnities for which the liturgical books contain a different set of prayers and scriptural readings for the Vigil Mass, the prime examples being Easter, Pentecost and Christmas. This continues the long tradition of independent texts for such celebrations that were also found in the Tridentine Missal.

In an enclosed religious environment, such as a seminary or monastery, where most of the community would attend a separate vigil celebration on a major feast as well as a liturgy on the day itself (as many people do at Easter), it makes perfect sense to use independent sets of scriptural readings at the different celebrations. But attendance at multiple Masses on Sunday or holy days is not a common practice in most parishes and, in parishes with no resident pastor, the community may be lucky to have a single Mass to celebrate a Sunday or feast!

Although churches are usually overflowing at Christmas Masses, usually only a small fraction of those present attend more than one liturgical celebration, particularly if there are small children in the family eager to open presents or play with new toys. For those individuals and families who attend the Christmas Vigil

Mass, the proclamation of the genealogy of Jesus and of Joseph's dream according to Matthew may not be as uplifting as the Lucan narrative of the Lord's birth.

A rubric found in the *Lectionary for Mass*, 13, where the scriptural texts for the Vigil Mass are found, notes that the texts given for the Vigil Mass may also be for Masses on Christmas Day. In addition, it permits choosing from any of the other three sets of readings "according to the pastoral needs of each congregation." Basically, the lectionary says that all four sets of readings (Vigil Mass, Midnight Mass, Dawn Mass, Day Mass) are interchangeable with the decision as to which readings to use at which Mass based on "pastoral needs."

Although all four Christmas Masses focus on the mystery of the Lord's birth, each celebrates this event in a slightly different way. Perhaps this is most readily seen in the focus on the Word made flesh via John's prologue in the Mass during Christmas Day. The mystery of Christ's birth is a reality that is bigger than just the story of Jesus being born and laid in a manger (the gospel for Mass at midnight). It is the mystery of God's love for the world (John 3:16), the mystery of Jesus being descended from Abraham and David (the gospel for the vigil), the mystery of the shepherds' hearing the proclamation of the angels and visiting the newborn infant (the gospel for dawn), the mystery of Emmanuel (again, the vigil's gospel), the mystery of the light that shines in the darkness (again, the gospel for Mass during the day).

Some places attempt to retain the distinctive character of each celebration, yet also try to include, in an appropriate way, the traditional Lucan biblical narrative of Christ's birth. For example, one parish might use part of the Lucan narrative as a "call to worship" before the entrance procession if another gospel is read during the liturgy of the word. Another parish may use part of the Lucan gospel to introduce the period of reflection after communion. If a parish schedules more than one Mass on Christmas Eve, one of the celebrations (geared toward families with small children) might use the Lucan gospel, while the others could use Matthew's genealogy.

It is easy to use the same readings at each of the Christmas Masses, and the lectionary does, in fact, permit this. But choosing that option can impoverish the celebration of the feast. It is more challenging to make use of the various sets of readings in the lectionary in such a way that the community as a whole becomes better aware of the multiple facets of this feast, as it celebrates God's love made visible in our world.

What is the rule for inserting additional names into the Litany of the Saints sung at the Easter Vigil? Can names of people who are not canonized saints be included? If the names of the candidates are, in fact, saints' names, should we include these?

Some background on litanies might be good to put their role in context. In its fundamental structure, any litany is a highly interactive sung prayer in which a deacon or cantor pronounces varying intentions (or invokes holy men and women of ages past) and the assembly responds with a standard phrase. (This "highly interactive" nature of a litany becomes obscured when the intentions become so long, that it becomes difficult to grasp what is being recommended for prayer, as can happen at the general intercessions at Mass.) In the case of the Litany of the Saints (or any similar litany, such as the Litany of the Blessed Virgin Mary), the bulk of it consists of names of individuals being invoked as intercessors for those at prayer. Since the church believes that saints fully share the life of the risen Christ, they are seen as ones who can be invoked by the entire church in a formal, public way, and invoked precisely as intercessors with God for the needs of those still living on earth.

The church has always exercised caution about devotion to saints and has discouraged *public* prayer even to people of virtuous life unless there has been a formal declaration that the individuals may be addressed as "blessed" or "saint" (an action called respectively "beatification" and "canonization") (see Code of Canon Law, 1187). This restriction should not be seen as casting doubts on the virtuous lives of people such as Mother Teresa, Dorothy Day, Oscar Romero or even our own grandparents or parents, but such a restriction does ensure that when the local community gathers for formal, public prayer, those to whom we pray as intercessors are individuals that the entire church feels comfortable in invoking.

On the private level, people can "pray" to anyone who has died since this is merely an extension of the biblically inspired practice of asking some other living person to pray for them (see 1 Thessalonians 5:25). If our belief in the "communion of saints" means anything, it means that death has not severed the bond in faith that we enjoyed during life and that Christian activities, such as praying for others, may also continue after someone has died.

The Litany of the Saints is used in the contemporary Roman liturgy as a moment of solemn prayer in conjunction with a significant action. Thus, during the rites of ordination, those to be ordained prostrate themselves immediately before the imposition of hands and the consecratory prayer. During this prostration, the assembly prays for the candidates and vocalizes their prayers through the singing of the Litany of the Saints.

But another traditional use of the litany is as a processional song. Hence, during the former devotion of the "Greater and Lesser Litanies," usually celebrated in April in the pre-1969 Roman calendar, the Litany of the Saints was sung in procession as a solemn way of asking the saints to intercede with God for divine blessings on the spring planting season. The current rubric for the Easter Vigil permits the Litany of the Saints to be used as a processional song (see RCIA [U.S. edition], 219) while those to be baptized move to the baptistry along with the ministers. This litany serves as a solemn moment of prayer by the community for the candidates, initially invoking the intercession of the saints, and then including invocations to Christ and a specific intention for the candidates. After the litany, the presider then introduces the prayer for the blessing of the water. Following this blessing, the candidates are questioned, baptized and confirmed.

If there is no procession to the baptistry, the litany is sung between the introduction to the prayer of blessing and the actual blessing of baptismal water, giving special emphasis to the solemn blessing. In either case it serves as a formal, highly participatory moment of prayer for the candidates, invoking the major figures of Christian history that the church publicly acknowledges as sharing in Christ's victory over sin and death.

The rubrics for the Easter Vigil explicitly mention that names of other saints may be added to the litany (2002 Roman Missal, rubric 43; see RCIA, 221), in particular the patrons of the candidates and the titular saints of the church. By referring to the patrons of the candidates, this rubric reflects the older practice that required Catholics to have Christian names, normally understood as names of canonized saints (1917 Code of Canon Law, 761). In addition to the common list of canonized saints, some religious institutes (for example, Benedictines, Franciscans, Jesuits) use a version of the Litany of the Saints that mentions the saints of the institute. In these litanies, the institute is permitted to include the names of those beatified but not yet canonized. This practice would recommend that the beatified of the country may be added, if there is local devotion to them. For example, North American communities might consider including the names of Blessed Kateri Tekakwitha or others beatified and remembered on the calendars of countries in North or South America. Thus it is not only permitted, but in a sense encouraged, to augment the list of saints' names to reflect the devotion of the local community and to relate the saints invoked to the action taking place.

Given the history of and norms governing the Litany of the Saints, what should be done if one of the candidates does not have what would be considered a "Christian" name? This may be a rare occurrence, considering all those who have been canonized over the centuries, but it still may occur, especially in the case of individuals who are not of European ancestry. (One should note that some "Christian" names may not directly be a name of a saint, such as "Alma" or "Assumpta," both of which are *titles* of Mary!)

In some situations, the parish staff may suggest an old option, namely, that a candidate consider choosing a "baptismal name," which would be the name of some saint the candidate holds in high regard. This is similar to the former custom of choosing a secondary "confirmation name." This name could be used by the candidate in addition to the given personal name, and the name of this saint could be used during the Litany of the Saints. Another option would be not to include any additional saints' names, which might be a good choice if the number of those to be baptized is large.

These options would address the practice of including patronal names of baptismal candidates within the litany. But what about adding the names of other holy men and women, generally honored by the local community but not formally canonized or beatified?

The present rubrics do not envision including the names of such individuals in the litany as people whom the community invokes in prayer. As noted above, since the litany is a formal, public prayer by the local church, one needs to respect the traditional caution about publicly praying to individuals, even those of remarkable virtue, without some sort of approbation by the shepherds of the church. Yet it may be possible to incorporate references to other individuals in the latter petitions. For example, if the local parish sponsors a Catholic Worker house, an appropriate intercession may be "Bless us with the vision of Dorothy Day to comfort those in need."

The Litany of the Saints is a traditional prayer form by which the community invokes those whom the church has publicly acknowledged as worthy of imitation and honor because of their heroic virtue. It must be honestly acknowledged that the list of saints included in the standard litany is dominated by European males, and thus is far from "catholic" (in the sense of universally inclusive)! It is tempting to augment the litany by including names of individuals honored by many contemporary Christians, and such augmentation is in fact permitted as noted above. But any such augmentation should be done carefully, lest the transformed litany no longer be primarily a litany of "saints" or, perhaps, the augmented list become a source of division during the celebration of a sacrament of unity.

Last Lent, a number of parents presented their young children on Ash Wednesday to receive ashes. I have mixed feelings about imposing ashes on infants and toddlers who have no consciousness about sin and repentance, and have no apparent need to "turn away from sin and believe in the good news." Do you have any suggestions?

When one surveys all the liturgical practices and traditions that comprise the liturgy of the Catholic church (particularly the traditions of the various Eastern churches and the non-Roman Western rites), one notices that there are a great variety of practices. Some exist that Western Catholics may find highly questionable, yet are held in high esteem in other traditions. For example, it is common in many Eastern churches to minister communion to infants. Sometimes this is accomplished by the priest dipping his finger into the chalice and then touching that finger to the child's lips. Some Western Catholics may find this practice bizarre and may object to it, usually basing their objection on the fact that infants have no consciousness of what is happening as they receive the eucharist.

Yet, every liturgical action is an action of the church, even though certain rites appear to be an interaction between two individuals—the Christian requesting the celebration of the ritual action and the minister. Thus the liturgy is never merely a private action, for the church is built up even through what may seem to many to be the passivity of silently witnessing a liturgical action. Therefore, in the case of the communion of infants, even though an infant may have no consciousness of the reality of what it receives as nourishment, the local church at prayer is built up by witnessing the action of the Lord nourishing all of his faithful, young as well as old.

But one should not arbitrarily impose the customs and piety of one segment of the church on another, whether it is Western customs on Eastern Christians or vice versa. (I am not advocating that the Western Church immediately start giving communion to infants in arms merely to imitate Eastern traditions.) There may be something for us to learn from Eastern liturgical traditions in addressing the appropriateness of imposing ashes on infants. And I suggest that what we can learn is that understanding a liturgical action in which a person is participating, while normally desirable, is not a *sine qua non* for the celebration of a sacrament or other liturgical rite.

The use of ashes as a sign of repentance, grief or mortality has a long religious tradition. We find references to ashes (sometimes with specific references to ashes on the head) in various places in the scriptures, for example, in the second book of Samuel (13:19), the book of Judith (4:11), the book of Esther (4:1, C:13), the book of Jonah (3:6) and the first book of Maccabees (3:47). Although there is no specific reference to children in such texts, some suggest an inclusivity regarding penitential practices. For example, in the first book of Maccabees, we read that "the assembly . . . sprinkled ashes on their heads and tore their clothes," and in Jonah, the king orders that "humans and beasts shall be covered with sackcloth." Texts such as these suggest that some penitential practices have value as signs to others and may not demand a conscious understanding of all the participants.

The Roman Missal itself offers little guidance regarding this question, since there is no reference to who should or should not receive ashes. The liturgical texts speak of the ashes as a "mark of our repentance," thus linking this rite to the biblical tradition of visibly showing to others one's own personal commitment to a change of lifestyle. With this in mind, it is appropriate for catechumens present at an Ash Wednesday liturgy to receive ashes, even though they have not been finally incorporated into the church through the sacraments of Christian initiation.

Perhaps a better place to look for guidance regarding what to do with small children in is the *Rite of Baptism for Children.*

There, the standard rite provides for an anointing with the oil of catechumens after a prayer of exorcism in which God's power is invoked to bring the children "out of the power of darkness" and to "strengthen them with the grace of Christ." The oil is applied after a formula that asks Christ to strengthen the child with his power. (This is parallel to the optional rite of anointing in the *Rite of Christian Initiation of Adults*.)

Though an infant is without culpability and understanding, it nevertheless does make sense to pray that children be kept safe from evil in the world, both its external effects and its internal, personal influences. It also makes sense to seek God's strength on behalf of the child. And this is what the prayer of exorcism and the anointing with oil are concerned with. The texts used in the Ash Wednesday rite acknowledge that ashes have a two-fold symbolism: They are symbolic of our frailty and mortality ("and to dust you shall return") as well as symbolic of reorienting our lives toward God's ways ("and believe in the good news"). In a sense, these thrusts are appropriate prayers or admonitions that can be addressed to people of all ages, the old as well as the very young. There is little in our world so heart-wrenching as the death of a small child, yet this is a reality that exists, and it can be a holy moment for families and communities to realize that even the youngest is not immune from the reality that "to dust [we] shall return." There is no one in our world who perfectly follows the teachings of Jesus, and so it can also be a holy moment for families and communities to realize that they must help everyone, including the youngest, to learn how to "believe in the good news."

The problem that does exist with a rite such as the distribution of ashes is that, in certain subcultures, it is overlaid with a piety that borders on superstition. Liturgical rites are actions of faith meant to nourish faith — they are never magic. Whether infants receive ashes or not is almost secondary to the question of whether the adults present receive this "sacramental" with faith, marking the beginning of a period of prayer and penance, rather than as an amulet that somehow makes them automatically holy.

I would not encourage parents to bring infants to be signed with ashes, but neither would I refuse to impose ashes on children if their parents present them.

The reception of ashes should never be seen as an end in itself, for it marks the beginning of the Western church's annual journey of prayer, penance and almsgiving in preparation for Easter. What is more important than the reception of ashes is full participation in the mystery of Christ's death and resurrection, a mystery to which we are intimately united through our baptism!

Last year, the neighboring parish reintroduced the veiling of statues and crosses in purple cloth during the last two weeks of Lent. Is this an option that is permitted and, thus, can be chosen by the local community?

Until 2002, the simple answer was, for the United States, "no." Perhaps some additional explanation may be appropriate and further comments helpful!

One of the great visual impacts associated with Lent and prescribed by the rubrics of the Tridentine Missal was the practice of covering crosses and statues during the last two weeks of Lent— from the Fifth Sunday of Lent (formerly known as "Passion Sunday I") until the singing of the Gloria at the Easter Vigil. This practice was one of the ways of marking the two weeks before Easter Sunday as a special time, a period called "Passiontide." (There were also less visible changes in the Mass during these two weeks, such as the omission of reciting the "Glory be" prayers whenever they appeared, and the omission of Psalm 43 during the prayers at the foot of the altar.)

The revision of the liturgical calendar that was promulgated in 1969 suppressed the former period of Passiontide by omitting any reference to it. The same revision restored the prominence of the Easter Triduum (not mentioned in the Tridentine Missal), which begins with the evening Mass of the Lord's Supper on Holy Thursday and ends with evening prayer on Easter Sunday (see *General Norms for the Liturgical Year and the Calendar* (GNLYC), 19). It also restored the special Easter fast associated with the Triduum, particularly on Good Friday and Holy Saturday (GNLYC, 20; see *Rite of Christian Initiation of Adults* [U.S. edition], 185.1). In addition, it explicitly determines that Lent ends with the start of the Mass of the Lord's Supper on Holy Thursday (GNLYC, 28).

Lent is now seen as one unified season that prepares for the celebration of the mysteries of our redemption during the Easter Triduum. Thus customs associated with the Tridentine Missal that highlight the two weeks before Easter Sunday and ignore the distinction between Lent and the Triduum are not in keeping with the revised liturgy and our renewed understanding of how to prepare for and celebrate Easter.

By no longer requiring that crosses and statues be veiled in purple, the revised Roman Missal has, in general, suppressed this former practice. But, in deference to countries that may have had a special attachment to this custom, the revised missal did permit national episcopal conferences to decide whether this practice of the Tridentine Missal could be continued in their countries. For the former practice to be retained, however, even optionally, it is necessary for the episcopal conference to take a formal vote on the practice. (One may remember that such votes had to be taken to permit communion in the hand in the United States, and to permit communion under both kinds on all weekdays and Sundays. An individual bishop could not allow such practices on his own initiative, much less a local pastor.)

As a matter of record, in the early 1970s the U.S. bishops' conference never voted to retain the practice of veiling statues and crosses during the last two weeks of Lent, either as a required or an optional practice. Thus, until 2002, parishes were technically not free to retain this practice or reintroduce it. This was noted in the *Newsletter of the Bishops' Committee on the Liturgy,* April 1995, p. 206.

Especially when personal preferences conflict with established regulations, I suggest it is important to move beyond the letter of any law to understand the spirit behind it. The revised missal and revised sacramental rites simplified many practices found in the Tridentine liturgical books. For example, no longer do we place salt on the tongues of those to be baptized. No longer must the presiding priest on Palm Sunday individually hand out blessed palm branches to everyone present at the blessing of palms: The revised missal states that those present should already have palms in their hands and that it is those branches that are blessed. Such simplification is also seen in the elimination of the mandatory practice of veiling statues and crosses.

Although it was a very dramatic part of the Easter Vigil, when, during the Gloria, the statues were suddenly uncovered, it was also distractingly humorous when a veil became snagged and would not come off as planned. In addition, in larger churches, it required a small army of servers to rush around the church trying to uncover numerous statues in a limited period of time in addition to lighting all the candles!

Furthermore, the practice of waiting until the Gloria of the Easter Vigil to unveil the statues of the church ignored the distinctive character of the Triduum as a whole. Now, in contrast, documents stress that Lent and the Triduum are distinct periods and they no longer mark the last two weeks of Lent in any special way.

The unity of the season of Lent was very much in the minds of two contemporary authors who advocated the revival of the custom of veiling statues. G. Thomas Ryan, writing in *The Sacristy Manual* (Chicago: LTP, 1993), and Peter Mazar, writing in *To Crown the Year* (Chicago: LTP, 1994), both suggested that if parishes veil statues during Lent, they should veil them before the Ash Wednesday liturgies and keep the veils in place for the whole season. Peter Mazar even gives some good pastoral and theological reasons why veiling sacred images at this time of year might be a good practice.

When the imminent publication of the third edition of the Roman Missal was announced in 2000, various suggestions were proposed to the U.S. Bishops' Committee on the Liturgy as possible adaptations for the United States. One such suggestion concerned the veiling of statues at the end of Lent. In June of 2001, the U.S. bishops' conference approved the veiling as an optional practice, and this decision was confirmed by Rome when the new edition finally appeared in Latin in March of 2002. Thus it is once again permitted (but not required) to veil the statues during the end of Lent in the United States.

Lent demands careful planning—for the catechumens, for the baptized, for music, for church environment and for all other aspects of the liturgy. The color of Lent is traditionally purple (violet) in the Roman rite. It is certainly appropriate to adorn the church, with an austerity appropriate to this penitential season, by using the color of purple. In some churches, purple bunting around shrines or purple banners in the sanctuary may lend an appropriate atmosphere. In other churches, subdued lighting of statues and images may add an appropriate somberness that can be more prayerful and dramatic than the use of purple cloth. In some places, it may even be appropriate to remove statues or icons during Lent, and return them before the beginning of the Triduum. In all cases, lenten decorations should never be more dramatic than those used during the Triduum and throughout the Easter season.

In order to highlight the difference between Lent and the Easter Triduum, it would also be very appropriate to remove all lenten decorations before the start of the Mass of the Lord's Supper on Holy Thursday (for example, when the holy water fonts are emptied). According to the Roman Missal, after the Mass of the Lord's Supper, crosses should be removed from the main body of the church or covered in red (the liturgical color of Good Friday).

There is much that can be done in terms of liturgical ambience to highlight our preparation for and celebration of the most important event of our faith: the death and resurrection of Christ! Certainly the veiling of statues may be appropriate in some communities, but this practice may also lead to a nostalgia that may confuse rather than cultivate a proper devotion to the celebration of the Triduum. My suggestion is that communities should look to new ways of arranging the worship environment, ways consistent with the starkness and simplicity of Lent and helpful in enhancing our renewed understanding of Lent, the Triduum and the 50 days of Easter. The ideal is to provide an ambience that is appropriate to our culture and age, supportive of the community's lenten prayer, and helpful in leading people from the ashes of Ash Wednesday to the fire of Christ's light and risen life.

Our Catholic school is in session on Holy Thursday. We know we cannot have Mass in the morning, and we also realize that morning prayer or a liturgy of the word would be good options to help to highlight the beginning of the Triduum. Yet we know that a good number of our students won't attend the whole Triduum, and maybe just Easter Sunday Mass. What might we do to lead them into the Triduum—to peak their interest a bit?

Preparing people properly so that they will want to participate fully in all of the liturgies of the Easter Triduum is an admirable goal and an ongoing challenge to the pastoral staff of any parish. One might want to make a special effort to draw certain groups (high school students, for example) to these liturgies. In some parishes, the liturgies of the Triduum are sparsely attended by people of all ages, even those who otherwise may attend weekday Masses regularly, particularly when comparing attendance to the Easter morning Masses, or to Masses on any given Sunday. Thus any attempt to plan something for students of a parish grammar school or of a local diocesan high school should be well integrated into wider plans that attempt to make all segments of a parish community eager about celebrating the liturgies of the Easter Triduum. It is unrealistic to think that students are going to attend the liturgies of the Easter Triduum if their parents are planning trips to visit relatives or mini-family-vacations and will be spending much of the Easter Triduum on the road.

Depending on what has happened during Lent, one option might be *not* to have any sort of prayer service with students on Holy Thursday morning. Rather than showing a lack of imagination, with proper catechesis, this option could highlight the importance of the evening liturgy of the Lord's Supper. Having a special liturgy of any length also runs the risk of suggesting to students that they have "already done their duty" of participating in a service that day, and may deter them from further participation. In addition, if Morning Prayer were celebrated with children only on Holy Thursday morning and not on any other day of the year, it might be understood as a special children's service for Holy Thursday, rather than as the daily prayer of the entire church throughout the year.

The gospels (see, for example, Matthew 26:17) record that the disciples asked Jesus about "preparing for the Passover." Perhaps better success would be achieved if, throughout the season of Lent, each and every liturgy were explicitly directed toward the celebration of the entire Easter Triduum. Any such service would then be understood as a kind of remote preparation for the three-day "Christian Passover." Good preparation can thus lead to good participation and good celebration. For example, even liturgies on Ash Wednesday can point to the Triduum if the assembly is reminded that in the world, fire leads to ashes, but in our faith, the ashes of the beginning of Lent lead to the fire of the Easter Vigil and the radiance of the light of Christ. Perhaps an explicit invitation (or challenge) should be made to the assembly on Ash Wednesday to undertake the disciplines of Lent in order to participate in the Triduum. Perhaps this invitation or challenge should name the dates and times of the Triduum liturgies. And certainly all preaching throughout Lent should be oriented toward celebrating the sacraments of initiation at the Easter Vigil.

There are no easy answers about what is able to peak the interest of children and adults and draw them to communal liturgical celebrations. We all know the drawing power of ashes, and how full many churches are on Ash Wednesday. Perhaps even though the revised rites of the Easter Triduum, first restored around 1955, have been with us for over 45 years, the piety of many people still has not shifted so that these liturgies have the same drawing power. Certainly, if done well, washing feet, kissing the cross, lighting a bonfire, sharing a flame, washing and anointing and welcoming to the table new members of Christ's body all can be very engaging and significant moments during the liturgies of the Triduum.

In some communities and among certain ethnic groups, there are popular customs associated with the Easter Triduum. For example, there is the practice of visiting the "altar of repose" in seven churches on the evening of Holy Thursday. Unfortunately, this devotion often substitutes for participation in the liturgy of the Lord's Supper. It can be a mixed blessing to create a new "tradition" meant to draw people to participate in the Triduum liturgies, only to find that the service or pious action actually decreases attendance at the official liturgies!

Without giving a direct answer as to what to do with school children on Holy Thursday morning, let me offer a few thoughts about preparation for the Easter Triduum.

1. No amount of preparation will work if the Triduum liturgies themselves are not celebrated well. The majority of energy in a parish should be spent in celebrating these three liturgies with dignity and grace. The washing of feet should only rarely be omitted; everyone in the church should venerate a single large cross; the Easter bonfire should be substantial and all should process from the fire (outside the church!) into the church building for the Exsultet, the readings, the baptismal liturgy and the eucharist.

2. If candidates and catechumens are well-known in the community, because they have been seen, prayed for and publicly dismissed during Lent, and if a general invitation is given to the parish to join these sisters and brothers in the final stage of their initiation at the Easter Vigil with a festive reception afterward, more members of the community may attend. Students in Catholic schools might be encouraged, throughout Lent, to pray for peers they know who may be initiated at the Easter Vigil and to join them in the celebration.

3. Homilies and images used throughout Lent might focus on some of the primary symbols of the Triduum, such as the cross, bread, water and light, among others. If members of the local community make the connection between certain basic symbols and the Triduum liturgies, they may be more likely to participate in these celebrations, as people already do on Ash Wednesday.

4. The paschal mystery is the mystery of life through death, the grain of wheat that bears fruit only because it dies. One may do damage to Christian tradition by focusing only on one aspect of this mystery and ignoring the other. Unfortunately, this can happen during Lent when devotions often focus exclusively on Christ's suffering and death and overlook the resurrection. Note that the official liturgical prayers on Good Friday keep the unity of the paschal mystery and mention Christ's resurrection. Thus it might be helpful, at least occasionally, to modify pious practices, such as the stations of the cross, to broaden the focus. One could do this by also including preliminary "stations" (such as the Last Supper, the Foot Washing, the Agony in the Garden) and conclude the stations with the proclamation of the gospels focusing on the Lord's resurrection or his appearance at Emmaus. In this way, aspects of the entire paschal mystery, from the Last Supper to the recognition of the risen Lord, can be previewed during Lent before the beginning of the Triduum.

Pastoral planners may want to learn a lesson from common practices used to publicize new movies (as much as I dislike using Hollywood as a model for liturgy). People don't flock to movies because of a lack of advertisements. Sometimes, previews occur in theaters several months before a movie is released and one sees these ads over and over again. One will probably not increase student attendance at Triduum liturgies by scheduling a single service immediately before the Triduum begins. Rather, people need to be alerted to the significance of these celebrations weeks and months in advance. These Triduum liturgies need to be celebrations that people will want to attend, not only because of the way they are celebrated, but also because of what they have come to learn the celebrations mean for their personal spiritual journeys.

Baptism and Confirmation

What are the requirements for godparents and confirmation sponsors?

Being chosen as a godparent (whether for baptism or for confirmation) is an honor, for the godparent is a person who traditionally becomes a companion to the one being baptized or confirmed, whether infant or adult, in a journey of faith. And the role of joining someone along the journey of faith, if taken seriously, can be both humbling as well as very awe-inspiring.

Godparents have a liturgical role in the rites of initiation, proclaiming their own faith (see *Rite of Christian Initiation of Adults* [U.S. edition], 53) and, in the case of infants, agreeing to assist the parents in raising the child in the Catholic faith (see *Rite of Baptism for Children*, 40). This is a solemn pledge, made publicly, and those who make such a pledge should be individuals whose standing in the community is such that credence can be given to the words they speak.

In the case of a child, up to a few decades ago, a godparent was assumed to be the one whose duty it was to raise a child "as a Catholic" in the unlikely event that the parents died or were unable to do so. Current church law recommends that the "godparent" of an infant also be the "sponsor" at that child's confirmation (see *Rite of Confirmation,* Introduction, 5; Code of Canon Law (CIC), 874, 892–893).

In the case of adults, the godparent (or sponsor) is someone who helps in the preparation of the adult and, after the adult has received the sacraments of initiation, continues to help the newly baptized in leading a life in harmony with Christian tradition, especially during the period of "mystagogy" (see RCIA [U.S. edition], 10–11, 246, 248).

Godparents should be both role models and mentors, individuals who are at ease with the practice of their faith and would normally be considered "active Catholics." They should be people who are comfortable with answering questions about their personal relationship with God as experienced in the Catholic communion, even if they are unsure about all of the technicalities. They should be people who are interested in and will continue to support their "godchild" in the years ahead as they and their godchild develop in their relationships with God and with other Catholic Christians.

Church law specifies that godparents (and confirmation sponsors) must be at least 16 years old (CIC, 874, section 1.2) and have been fully initiated, that is, that they have celebrated the sacraments of baptism, confirmation and eucharist, and are living a life consistent with the office undertaken (CIC, 874, section 1.3; see CIC, 872–873; *Rite of Confirmation,* Introduction, 5–6). It also assumes that godparents have been asked to serve in this role by the individual to be baptized (or, in the case of infants, by the family or, if they do not know anyone, the local pastor) (see CIC, 874, section 1.1). The other requirements stipulate that parents should not be godparents (CIC, 874, section 1.5), nor should anyone whose church status is questionable (CIC, 874, sections 1.3–1.4).

The role of godparent or sponsor is not merely that of patron, but that of mentor. And so, sometimes emotional conflicts occur in a family when relatives or close friends who are held in esteem are considered as possible godparents but are technically not qualified either because they are not Catholic, they don't practice their faith regularly or their religious status is "problematic" because of some situation (for example, they might have had a civil marriage without a sacramental one).

It is occasionally permitted for a non-Catholic Christian to be associated as a "Christian witness" to a baptism (see CIC, 874, section 2). Though not officially a godparent, such an individual can still function as a role model for someone who is trying to learn about how a person should follow Christ in our troublesome world. In such situations, another person should be designated as the official godparent, someone who fits the traditional categories.

Most people are aware of the conflicts that can occur between loyalties based on friendship and the demands of liturgical and religious authenticity. Baptism and confirmation are sacraments of faith, and the major ministers, including the godparents and sponsors, should be examples of faith for those gathered in prayer. Not every relative or friend is appropriate to serve as godparent and not every person who is appropriate as a godparent is close enough to serve in that capacity. Balance is not easy to achieve! In special cases, the advice and wisdom of the local priest or pastoral minister can be very helpful.

We have a new immersion baptismal font in our recently renovated church. Is it appropriate for the minister of baptism to stand in the font along with the candidate being baptized?

Several factors in the last few decades have happily converged to bring about changes in the ways that baptisms are celebrated. One factor was the revision of the rites of infant baptism and of adult initiation. In both of these orders, baptism "by immersion" is mentioned as the first of the options to be used for the sacramental washing. Another factor is the widespread vitality of catechumenates with an increase in adult baptisms as part of a public liturgy. A third factor is a rediscovery of the importance of symbol in liturgical rites and a realization that baptism by immersion conveys a depth of the image of burial with Christ that baptism by pouring does not (see *Rite of Christian Initiation of Adults,* Introduction, 22).

In response to a desire to enable baptism to be celebrated by immersion, newer churches and renovated churches have included fonts in which candidates, whether they are adults or children, may actually enter into the waters of baptism. This raises the issue of where the minister of baptism should be when performing the sacramental washing.

Since Western Catholics have only relatively recently reintroduced the practice of performing the sacramental washing of baptism by immersion rather than by pouring, we have no traditions about how to celebrate baptism by immersion in memory. Some Eastern Catholics in the United States unfortunately abandoned the Eastern tradition of baptism by immersion, and others use an immersion font only for infants. So, in trying to develop a practice, some priests and deacons have looked to those Western Christian denominations that have long practiced baptism by immersion and have experience in baptizing adults.

Such churches frequently have a large pool into which the minister and candidate both enter into about waist-deep waters. Afterward, the minister baptizes the candidate by leaning the candidate (usually backwards) three times into the waters of the font.

Unfortunately, detailed descriptions of baptisms from early centuries usually neglect to mention anything about the location of the minister and mention little else other than the fact that the candidate somehow entered the waters of the font. At least one ancient text suggests that the minister did not enter the water, while another suggests that the minister was in the font with the candidate. Excavations of early Christian worship spaces have shown that many fonts were not very deep or very large. Some had three steps inside (perhaps symbolic of three days in the tomb). Some were cruciform in shape with steps at the ends of the cross bar, suggesting that the candidates entered at one end and exited at the other.

Because the historical data does not unambiguously answer all questions and since contemporary practice should not merely duplicate fourth-century practice, it might be good to reflect on what should be highlighted in symbol in celebrating the central sacramental action of baptism.

The core action is one in which a minister of the church (ordinarily a bishop, presbyter or deacon), a person who has already "passed" through the saving waters of baptism, elicits a commitment to faith from the candidate (or the parents of an infant) and then leads that fellow human being through the experience of Christ's death and resurrection symbolically through immersion. If one has already walked through the waters (symbolic of the people of Israel walking through the Red Sea and the Jordan River), should one ever walk through them again? What is the meaning of a minister repeatedly entering the waters if we say that this experience should be a once-in-a-lifetime event?

Then there are the questions of how deep the font should be—deep enough for submersion or merely for immersion? Trying to weigh different options and the values they each have is not easy. Let me suggest some points to consider, and offer some points to assist practice.

Historical data suggests that many ancient "immersion fonts" enabled someone to enter waters no more than knee deep and perhaps to be able kneel in the waters. Such fonts do not seem large enough for adult candidates to be completely submerged. It is possible that a candidate knelt when the sacramental formula was pronounced and more water was poured on him or her.

It also seems that in most places the minister usually remained outside the baptismal pool. Having entered the waters once, the minister did not enter them again, even to initiate a fellow Christian.

Such historical data, however, should by no means rigidly determine our baptismal practices. The church's liturgical praxis has and continues to develop as we gain new insights and adapt to our ever-changing world. What's important is a fundamental continuity of what is central to the liturgical rites and an appreciation for the symbols that each rite traditionally employs.

The challenge with baptism is to highlight the washing of the candidate with water. Some suggest that the focus on the candidate is compromised when a minister enters the font with the candidate. The challenge with baptism is to see the sacramental washing as an entry into the mystery of Christ's death and resurrection. A candidate entering a font and getting significantly wet images this better.

The font is womb and tomb. Baptism is death and rebirth, return to the garden of Eden, passage though the sea, union to Christ. We enter the waters once because God's promise is forever. The rites we use should be symbolically significant and faithful to tradition, and helpful for the candidate to experience all that baptism is meant to be.

When celebrating confirmation, do we need to provide ministers linen cloths with which to blot the foreheads of the newly confirmed as they move away from the bishop?

Before the revision of the rites that was mandated by the Second Vatican Council, it was common practice for assisting priests to wipe away the chrism that the bishop had just placed on the foreheads of those confirmed. But this was not merely a pious custom derived from reverence toward the sacred chrism. It was actually prescribed by the rubrics of the former *Rite of Confirmation.* In fact, it was given as an alternative to the original practice, that of tying a linen cloth around the head of the one confirmed so that the cloth covered the spot on the forehead where the oil remained (almost like a sweatband).

Nowhere in the introduction to the current *Rite of Confirmation* or in the rubrics themselves do we find any reference to these former practices. Because these former practices were not included in the revised confirmation rite, they should be considered to be suppressed and, therefore, should not be reintroduced.

In fact, because of our renewed and heightened sensitivity to the symbols of the liturgy, it is in a sense preferable that the bishop be somewhat generous in using chrism for the anointing and that those confirmed experience the moistness of the oil and the sweet-smelling fragrance that it emits. It is more respectful of our liturgical symbols to let the oil make an impact on the one confirmed, and it is better than immediately pretending that the anointing never happened by trying to remove any trace of it. Besides, it is simply more natural to rub ointment in than to wipe it off.

We can also be guided by the sound advice found in the pastoral notes for another sacrament that uses oil, the sacrament of the anointing of the sick. In the *Pastoral Care of the Sick,* we read the following: "If the anointing is to be an effective sacramental symbol, there should be a generous use of oil so that it will be seen and felt by the sick person as a sign of the Spirit's healing and strengthening presence. For the same reason, it is not desirable to wipe off the oil after the anointing" (107).

God gives the gift of the Spirit generously to all, and the Spirit is with us always as a companion and guide, to sanctify and to strengthen, enabling us to pray, "Abba" (Galatians 4:6). The generous yet reverent use of oil during the celebration of confirmation—and its lingering presence on those confirmed—should reflect the reality that we celebrate.

Some of our candidates for confirmation are asking about choosing a "confirmation name," since their parents or other relatives suggested the practice to them. Should we encourage this practice today in light of what we understand about baptism?

We cannot look at the pros and cons of choosing separate "confirmation names" without reflecting on names in a more general human and religious context, and particularly on the name used at baptism.

Personal names are realities that many people quite often take for granted. Yet, parents frequently spend many hours in deliberation when choosing a name for a newborn. Sometimes a child is named to honor another relative. Sometimes a child is named after a saint held in high esteem by the family. Sometimes a person has a special nickname used only by close relatives. Whatever the origin of our names, they become part of our history and identity.

Names are important in our religious tradition as well. The prophet Isaiah proclaims to King Cyrus that God "called you by your name" (Isaiah 45:3–4), and after the resurrection it was only when Jesus called Mary Magdalen by name that she recognized him (John 20:16).

Our personal names are used at our baptism and become part of our religious history. For many centuries, it was customary only to use the names of saints at baptism, but the baptismal rite now permits other names as long as they are not incompatible with Christian faith. The *Rite of Christian Initiation of Adults* (U.S. edition) even provides a rite for a catechumen to receive a "Christian" name before baptism (202).

Since confirmation is now seen in relationship to baptism, any discussion of a confirmation name must be placed in the context of the relationship of confirmation to baptism. Confirmation is seen as a "seal" of the faith and grace given in baptism. The current rite of confirmation tries to link the celebration of this sacrament of initiation to baptism and recommends that the sponsor for confirmation be, whenever possible, the baptismal godparent. It also includes a formal renewal of baptismal promises after the homily.

Since the rite contains no specific directive otherwise, it presumes that those to be confirmed will be addressed by the name used at their baptism. Choosing a separate confirmation name had been a centuries-old custom for those baptized as infants but confirmed later, but this practice emphasizes a separation between the two sacraments that is at variance with our renewed understanding of the inter-relationship of baptism, confirmation and eucharist as the three sacraments of Christian initiation. And, although popular in many places, in actuality "confirmation names" as such are mentioned nowhere in the former or current rite, or in the Code of Canon Law.

Thus there is no obligation to use a name at confirmation that is distinct from the name given at baptism, although the local bishop may find the older custom appropriate for educational and inspirational purposes.

We do find references to confirmation names in the history of the church, however. For example, Saint Adalbert (tenth century) actually received the name "Adalbert" at his confirmation. Under the guidance of Saint Charles Borromeo (sixteenth century), a diocesan council in Milan recommended that someone whose name was "unbecoming for a Christian" should receive another at confirmation. But this good advice was never an absolute requirement, and does not address the situation where someone's baptismal name is that of a canonized saint.

Taking a new name can be symbolic of a new stage in life, and we remember there is a biblical history of individuals who had their names changed: Abram to Abraham, Jacob to Israel, Simon to Peter. This precedent was one underlying reason why members of many religious orders chose "religious" names when pronouncing vows. But the celebration of confirmation is a time to reaffirm one's baptism, and thus should not been seen so much as a new stage of Christian life but as an opportunity to deepen the graces of baptism.

Celebrating the sacrament of confirmation can be an opportunity for candidates to reflect on what baptism and union with Christ should mean in their lives. It can also be a moment in which the candidates reflect on how they should live out their baptismal commitments in the future, imitating holy men and women of previous ages.

There may be, however, appropriate and pastoral reasons for someone to choose another patron saint and use this saint's name when being confirmed. This name, freely chosen and reflective of the candidate's devotion to a saint, can be a sign of commitment to living as a Christian in today's world under the patronage of someone they admire. Ideally such a confirmation name would be used in addition to the baptismal name, and not in place of it, and would be a saint to whom the person being confirmed has a particular devotion. On the other hand, for most individuals, using the baptismal name alone can be a powerful reaffirmation of who they are as Christians.

Whether a person chooses a special patron (and name) at confirmation or chooses to honor the name received at baptism, this should always be considered as a secondary aspect of the celebration. What is ultimately being celebrated is God's commitment to each baptized Christian through the gift of the Holy Spirit, a reality that should never be overshadowed, no matter which name is used!

Marriage

When is it appropriate to celebrate a wedding at Mass? At a liturgy of the word?

The *Constitution on the Sacred Liturgy* decreed that a marriage between Catholics should normally take place during Mass (78), and the 1969 revised *Rite of Marriage* also permitted a marriage between a Catholic and a baptized non-Catholic to be celebrated during Mass. These documents set the stage for contemporary Catholic marriage customs. Many have forgotten that before the Second Vatican Council, marriages between Catholics most often were not celebrated with a Mass and, when they were, the exchange of vows took place at the foot of the altar immediately before the prayers with which Mass began. Marriages between Catholics and non-Catholics were normally celebrated in the sacristy or the parlor of the rectory rather than in a Catholic church. Moreover, marriages were rarely celebrated during the seasons of Lent and Advent.

The Council envisioned an ideal and provided a corrective to what had been the common practice at that time. The post-conciliar marriage rite, however, provides several forms for celebrating marriage, and which form is chosen for which situations should depend on pastoral circumstances.

The choice of whether to have a wedding within a Mass or a liturgy of the word is sometimes based on relatively few (and somewhat trivial) considerations. The following are some examples: "Our best friends had a Mass at their wedding," "My parents want us to have a Mass at our wedding," "We don't want a long church ceremony so we can get to the reception sooner." The shortage of priests, however, is also an issue in this discussion, sometimes determining whether the wedding will be at a Mass, with a priest presiding, or at a liturgy of the word, with a deacon presiding. The priest's workload is another question: Is he expected to preside at perhaps two or three wedding Masses on a Saturday as well as at the Saturday evening Mass?

For a couple, both of whom are practicing Catholics and who have chosen a day for their wedding that does not coincide with a major feast on the liturgical calendar, it is most appropriate that their exchange of wedding vows take place in the context of a eucharistic celebration with the liturgical texts taken from the many options for a nuptial Mass. In this way, the sacrament of marriage, with its life of joys and sorrows, may be seen as one of the many possible reflections of the paschal mystery of Christ's life, death and resurrection. This is the ideal envisioned by Vatican II.

On the other hand, there may be numerous reasons that suggest a Mass is not the most appropriate context in which to celebrate a marriage. Some reasons may be called "internal" and others "external."

Internal reasons come from the situation of the couple being married. For example, if one of the spouses is not a Catholic, that spouse (and his or her family) would not normally be permitted to receive communion at the Mass. This visible sign of disunity may be very jarring if it were to be juxtaposed with all the symbols of union that are part of the entire wedding day. It may even be that both spouses are Catholics but are not regular in the practice of their religion. Hence, a celebration of the eucharist may be considered inappropriate by them and even by family and friends present. It should also be noted that even though the marriage rite permits a Mass at a wedding between a Catholic and a baptized non-Catholic, no such permission is given when the non-Catholic is not baptized. Thus, in general, if there is some circumstance that arises with the couple that would lead to a significantly less-than-ideal celebration of the eucharist (for example, a situation where the majority of those present would be silent spectators instead of active participants, or where one or both of the couple would not be receiving communion), it would be preferable to celebrate the marriage in the context of a liturgy of the word instead of a Mass.

External reasons arise from the day on which the wedding is scheduled. According to norms, ritual Masses, which include the wedding Mass, are not permitted on solemnities or their equivalents (for example, Sundays of Advent, Lent or Easter, Ash Wednesday, All Souls Day, Holy Week and the Octave of Easter) (see the 2002 *General Instruction of the Roman Missal*, 372). Thus, if there is to be a Mass, the Mass of the day (with its own readings) should be used (1969 Introduction of the *Rite of Marriage*, 11, and the 1990 Introduction, 34). For some reason, a couple may decide to be married, for example, on All Souls Day (November 2) or on a Sunday during the Easter season. On these days, the Mass of the day (for example, a Mass of the Dead on November 2) is to be used, but these texts do not provide the most appropriate context during which to exchange marriage vows. On days like these, it may be appropriate to forgo Mass and, instead, to celebrate the wedding within a liturgy of the word with the wedding scripture texts and prayers.

Certainly, the exchange of wedding vows during Mass is an ideal to which every couple and parish should strive, all other conditions being fulfilled. But that ideal is not an absolute, and there are often very good reasons why certain marriages are more appropriately celebrated at a liturgy of the word. This does not mean that the ritual being celebrated should be brief or perfunctory, however. It should always be celebrated with a dignity and festiveness appropriate to the mystery of divine and human love.

Who should be in the wedding procession, and in what order?

Since 1969, the current *Rite of Marriage* has stated: "If there is a procession to the altar, the ministers go first, followed by the priest, and then the bride and bridegroom. According to local custom, they may be escorted by at least their parents and the two witnesses. Meanwhile, the entrance song is sung" (20).

The Roman rite is sensitive to local custom, but it presents a model in which we see certain values. In my mind, some of the values enshrined here are (1) the equality of the spouses (both bride and groom enter together), (2) the equality of both parents (both mother and father join both spouses) and (3) the integration of the "bridal" procession into the traditional entrance procession of the Mass.

The second printing of the Canadian edition of the marriage rite (published in the mid-1970s) explicitly states in its pastoral notes that the opening procession described in the ritual should be the standard model followed in Canada. It mentions that the older procession, in which the bride with her female attendants is accompanied by her father and processed through the center aisle of the church while the priest, groom and male attendants wait in the sanctuary, is not mentioned in the ritual and had not been approved as an alternative by the Canadian bishops.

There is little to be said in favor of the so-called "traditional" bridal entrance. It can be rightly criticized for perpetuating the image that the bride is the property of her father, who alone has the right to "give her away" to another man (the groom). Using such an image is a poor way to start a marriage and is not an ideal practice to incorporate into a contemporary Catholic liturgy, which celebrates the equality of all people before God. From a ritual point of view, such a bridal entrance detracts from the structure and flow of the opening rites. Our tradition is to begin with the entrance procession of the ministers (if not the whole assembly as on Palm Sunday or at the Easter Vigil), with all giving voice to a common hymn and thus being united into the body of Christ. To stand and watch a parade is foreign to our sense of liturgy. And since the bride and groom are the principal ministers of the sacrament of marriage, why not have them enter as ministers of the liturgy usually do?

But old customs die hard. And moments as emotion-filled (and tradition-bound) as weddings are times when good liturgical practices are ignored in deference to traditions found in wedding manuals that know nothing of Catholic liturgical principles. Although the wedding is a special moment for the bride and groom, the liturgy should always be arranged so that it is a celebration of the entire community with and for the couple being wed. Unfortunately, weddings are often planned as if the worship of God is secondary to the attention given to the bride and groom.

People have adjusted well to other changes in the liturgy over the years and, in fact, now accept them as normal and good. Wedding customs should reflect our current understanding of what the liturgy should be and also reflect our current Sunday practices. If the ministers of the liturgy walk down the aisle from the church's entrance on Sundays, that should also be the practice at wedding Masses. If the parish stresses gender equality in its choice of ministers, then the wedding entrance procession should include both male and female attendants, as well as both parents of both the bride and the groom.

Even though television and movies perpetuate the traditional bridal entrance procession, I think the practice should be relegated to museums. The procession suggested by the ritual should become the standard practice in Catholic churches.

Where should the bride and groom stand during the exchange of vows? Should the bride and groom kneel throughout the wedding liturgy?

In the 1614 *Roman Ritual,* the exchange of consent occurred immediately *before* the nuptial Mass, and the rubrics specifically noted that the bride and groom should kneel before the altar with the priest facing them. In the 1969 *Rite of Marriage,* the rubrics (23) specifically noted that all should *stand* for the exchange of consent and rings, "including the bride and groom." But the rite does not give any further guidance about *where* the bridal couple should stand during the exchange of consent vis-à-vis the presiding priest or deacon, or where they should be during the rest of the liturgy. The rubrics leave such details to local practices and traditions, some of which may be determined by the physical surroundings of the liturgical space (for example, the floor plan of the church or the space available in the sanctuary).

A couple of suggestions may offer some guidance, however. The *Rite of Ordination* suggests that chairs for the ordinandi should be arranged "so that the faithful may have a complete view of the liturgical rites." Applying the same principle to the marriage liturgy, it is appropriate that the bride and groom have seats in the sanctuary (since they exercise a unique ministry in the sacrament of marriage), but their seats should be located so as not to block the view of others present of the central action of giving praise to God around the table of the Lord. Thus, this principle would generally preclude placing the couple at kneelers set right before the altar. The couple should be seated together, and their chairs could be located near the priest (but not in a way to compromise the presidential role of the priest), in some open space in the sanctuary enabling them to see the ambo and the altar or in some other place that enables them to be seen but also permits them the "full, conscious, and active participation" demanded by the *Constitution on the Sacred Liturgy* (14). On the other hand, it may be the custom in some parishes (for example, those in which the altar is located in the middle of the assembly) for the bridal couple to have special seats in the assembly and move to a more central and visible location for the actual exchange of consent.

The 2002 *General Instruction of the Roman Missal* speaks about a "uniformity in posture" being "observed by all participants" as "a sign of the unity of the members of the Christian community gathered for the sacred liturgy" (42). Thus, if the bride and groom (and any attendants) have places in the sanctuary for the marriage ceremony, they should be provided with appropriate chairs at which they can sit attentively during the liturgy of the word and be able to face the ambo while the reader proclaims the word of God. Kneelers should also be available for the couple and any attendants for the eucharistic prayer (if that is the local custom). Such kneelers, however, would not normally be placed before the altar since, when the couple would stand (as they should!) during the preface and the Lord's Prayer, for example, the location of the couple at the kneelers would interfere with the assembly's view of the altar.

For the actual exchange of consent and rings, it would be most appropriate for the couple and the witnesses to move to a location where they can readily be seen and easily be heard. Usually this means standing in front of the altar or even in the central aisle. The space should be large enough so that at least the two witnesses can be near the bridal couple, if not the other attendants as well.

It also seems appropriate that the witnesses and other attendants *not* be seated in the sanctuary during the entire liturgy, since they are needed only during the actual exchange of consent. By keeping the wedding attendants away from the sanctuary, the liturgical role of the bride and groom is heightened and the focus on the bridal couple is not diluted by numerous attendants, who in many cases may not be baptized persons and could become a distraction because of their lack of participation in the liturgy.

If the witnesses and other attendants were to be seated with the rest of the assembly, they could come to the appropriate location after the homily and return to their seats for the general intercessions, appropriately highlighting the central moment of the exchange of consent.

Although some priests position themselves with their backs to the assembly during the exchange of consent so that the faces of the bridal couple can more readily be seen by the assembly, I prefer that the priest stand so that he faces the assembly as the one who presides over its prayer, and that he ask the couple to face each other for the exchange of consent and of the rings. In this way, family and friends have an unimpeded view of the bride and the groom, who are committing themselves to each other at this key moment in the liturgy. The rubrics also prescribe that the bridal couple join their right hands during the consent as a symbol of the legal ramifications of the words being spoken, and this is only possible if the couple are actually facing each other at this time.

In a large sanctuary, if the couple is seated on one side of the altar, they might remain there during the eucharistic prayer and also for the nuptial blessing after the Lord's Prayer. In such a location, their faces would be visible to the assembly throughout the liturgy of the word and the liturgy of the eucharist. During the nuptial blessing, the priest could come to them and, perhaps, stand to their side as he invokes God's blessings on their married life.

Although the 1969 *Rite of Marriage* has been in use for over 30 years, too often the "choreography" used is the same as was used for the previous rite that had been published in the 1600s without any thought about the implications of the liturgical renewal of Vatican II! The principles of "full and active participation" and uniformity in posture apply to all in the assembly, including the bridal couple and their attendants, and apply to all liturgical services, wedding liturgies as well as Sunday Masses. Engaged couples, parish liturgy committees, wedding coordinators, priests and deacons all need to reflect on how well the ideal of good liturgy is realized or (unfortunately) compromised in the weddings in which they are involved!

Who should serve as ministers of communion and lectors at the wedding Mass? Is it appropriate for the bride and groom to do so?

In many ways, some of the customs still associated with weddings would be more appropriate for a pre–Vatican II marriage liturgy than for a wedding celebrated according to the 1969 *Rite of Marriage* and integrated into the 1969 *Order of Mass*. In particular, it is still too common for the bridal couple to spend hours pondering how many attendants (in addition to the official witnesses, that is, the best man and the maid of honor) should be part of the ceremony, and who should be chosen to be the bridesmaids and groomsmen.

Since a Catholic wedding ceremony is an official liturgical rite, decisions pertaining to participants who play a major role in the rite should be made according to Catholic liturgical principles. Unfortunately, such decisions are often made based on what is recommended by wedding magazines and books inspired by secular customs and authored by those who may have no concept of what should be proper practice at a Catholic wedding.

Every Catholic wedding now includes a formal proclamation of the word of God, and the person or persons who proclaim the biblical passages perform a significant liturgical ministry, which is much more important than being an auxiliary bridesmaid or groomsman. If the wedding is to take place during Mass and auxiliary ministers of the eucharist are needed, those who minister the Lord's body and blood to those assembled are also involved in a very significant ministry.

My advice (unpopular as it may be) is that the bridal couple limit the number of attendants to as few as possible (ideally, only the two witnesses), and invite other close friends and relatives to exercise the various roles of ministry open to them during the wedding rite.

Those chosen for the role of reader or eucharistic ministry (or any other liturgical ministry) should be familiar with the role and should normally perform this ministry at their home parishes. It is inappropriate to ask friends or relatives to serve in such major liturgical roles who are unfamiliar with these roles or, perhaps, do not practice their faith regularly.

On occasion, one may see a wedding at which the bride and groom also serve as eucharistic ministers, or perform some other liturgical function. Such a practice calls for further reflection.

The 2002 *General Instruction of the Roman Missal* (GIRM) gives some general principles about liturgical roles and expresses the preference for keeping roles distinct. For example, paragraph 59 notes that proclaiming the scripture is a ministerial rather than a presidential function and, thus, the presiding priest should not proclaim the gospel if a deacon or another priest is present. We find a similar recommendation that, if there are two readings, it is better to have two different readers fulfill the ministry of proclaiming the scripture (2002 GIRM, 109). The principle underlying such norms is that liturgical authenticity is compromised when a single person performs different roles.

It is the solemn duty of the bride and groom to express before the gathered assembly their consent (the "vows"). In a special way, they are being ministered to by others present who witness the couple's commitment being expressed and who minister to them in other ways. The scripture readings being proclaimed should be particularly addressed to the bride and groom; for this reason, it would seem odd for either to proclaim a reading.

Similarly, the reception by the bridal couple of the "one bread and one cup" should be a moment expressing the unity that their wedding signifies. The importance of this moment can be compromised if they are busy preparing to minister the consecrated elements to their invited guests.

In addition to the liturgical reasons, there may be practical reasons for the bridal couple to refrain from filling several roles at their own wedding. Often, a couple does not realize how nervous they may be until the ceremony begins. It is often better for the couple to remain at their places during the readings or the communion procession of the assembly and reflect in a somewhat relaxed manner on what has occurred, rather than be "present" to their assembled guests in yet another way.

A wedding liturgy is an occasion of great joy and also of significant emotion. It is fundamentally an action of praise and worship of our God, occasioned by the public commitment of the bride and groom, in love, to each other. Since this is a time of the community's prayer, it is most appropriate that those who regularly assist the Christian community as ministers (of the word or of the eucharist) serve in this fashion at the wedding liturgy. I would also suggest that it would be better if the bride and groom were to focus their ministry on their public proclamation of their nuptial consent rather than attempt to assume additional ministries during this liturgy. What's most important at a wedding rite is that God's love, visible in the life, death and resurrection of Christ, become visible in the commitment of the bridal couple for each other, and be celebrated in deep faith and with great joy!

If a deacon assists at a wedding Mass, may he preside over the exchange of vows? If so, is this a good idea?

As long as a deacon has received proper delegation to receive the consent of the bride and the groom, the rite itself does not explicitly prohibit him from receiving the consent, even though this may occur during a Mass celebrated by a priest. But, as Saint Paul suggests, not everything that is lawful is good or constructive (see 1 Corinthians 6:12; 10:23).

The liturgical books presuppose a certain model for liturgical celebrations. Normally, the celebration is presided over by a bishop (see the 2002 *General Instruction of the Roman Missal* [GIRM], 92) or, in his absence, a priest. Other ministers—specifically the deacon and readers—have their proper, assigned roles. Normally, a deacon does not fulfill a presidential role when a bishop or priest is present (see the *Book of Blessings* [BB], Introduction, 18c). Similarly, a layperson should not preside at a liturgical service (such as a blessing) when a priest or deacon is present (see BB, Introduction, 18d). The liturgical books also presuppose that only one person exercises the presidential office throughout a liturgical celebration (see 2002 GIRM, 108).

Only rarely is this practice altered. For example, in particular situations, a bishop is permitted to assign a priest to preside at the liturgy of the eucharist at Mass while he himself presides at the liturgy of the word and at the concluding rite (see 2002 GIRM, 92). And at the ordination of a new diocesan bishop in his cathedral, the newly ordained bishop may lead the assembly during the liturgy of the eucharist, taking over the presidency from the ordaining bishop. At other times, however, there should be only one leader of prayer throughout a single liturgical celebration.

Nevertheless, given the realities of our contemporary world (including a limited number of priests ministering to a growing number of the faithful), the ideal presented in the liturgical books may sometimes be prudently accommodated to the actual situation.

For example, although a bishop should preside at Mass when present, it is not uncommon at some funerals to see a bishop attending the Mass vested in choir robes, and a priest relative or religious superior of the deceased leading the assembly in prayer.

The 1990 revised Introduction to the *Rite of Marriage* notes in paragraph 23 that it "is preferable that the same priest prepare the engaged couple, give the homily during the celebration of the sacrament, receive the spouses' consent, and celebrate the Mass." There are many situations in which parishes are without a resident priest and a deacon may be the parish administrator and the one who leads the marriage preparation program. In such situations, it would be appropriate for the deacon who has pastoral responsibility for the local community (and has been entrusted with the preparation of the wedding couple) to preach during the nuptial Mass and receive the consent of the couple, rather than a visiting priest.

There may be other situations at which it would be appropriate for a deacon to receive the consent of the wedding couple during a nuptial Mass. A prime example would be when the deacon is a relative or close friend of either family.

This question provides one example of how we need to honor basic liturgical principles, yet also realize that there may be special situations that admit of exceptions to standard practices. It would be contrary to liturgical principles for parish deacons always to receive the consent of bridal couples during nuptial Masses celebrated by the parish priests. It would also seem contrary to common sense to prohibit the father or the brother of the bride or the groom from receiving the vows of his relative during a nuptial Mass. Whatever choice is made in any particular case, it should always respect liturgical tradition as well as exhibit prudence and sensitivity towards those present.

What are the pastoral and canonical implications of celebrating weddings at regularly scheduled Sunday Masses?

By their very nature, every sacrament is a celebration of the church, even if the community present consists of a priest and one other person, as commonly happens with the private celebration of the sacrament of penance. Sacraments should never be seen as the celebration of a small group of people who occasionally may permit others to attend. Great strides have been made in the understanding of the communal nature of the sacrament of baptism, for example, because of the practice in many parishes of regularly celebrating the baptism of infants during Sunday Mass and of encouraging everyone in the parish to witness the baptism of adults at the Easter Vigil.

The celebration of the sacrament of marriage, however, remains problematic in many places, with respect to its communal nature. People still tend to use the paradigm of a wedding that is commonly seen in Hollywood movies or on TV rather than what is envisioned by the Roman Ritual. Too often, the bride and groom refer to the ceremony as "our wedding," which, although a valid statement, portrays a mindset that divorces the wedding ritual from the larger faith community.

Most people assume that when a wedding takes place during Mass, the nuptial Mass and associated readings will be used, but this need not be the case. Although the sacrament of marriage can be celebrated any day of the year other than Good Friday and Holy Saturday, the celebration of a nuptial Mass is prohibited on a number of days, including solemnities, the Sundays of Advent, Lent and Easter, Holy Week and Easter Week (see 2002 GIRM, 372; the *Rite of Marriage,* 1969 Introduction, 11, and the 1990 Introduction, 32). On such days, the Mass of the day is celebrated with its proper readings, but the wedding rite is incorporated in the usual way (see the *Rite of Marriage,* 1990 Introduction, 34, and the *Ceremonial of Bishops,* 603). By not permitting the texts of the nuptial Mass on such days, the liturgical norms are pointing out that the observance of a major feast, celebrated in common by the broader church, takes precedence over a family event, and family sacramental events always need to be harmonized with the spirit and flow of the liturgical calendar. There is no such prohibition on Sundays in Ordinary Time, however, so it is possible to use the texts of a nuptial Mass on such Sundays, but only if the celebration does not take place at a usually scheduled parish Mass (see the *Rite of Marriage,* 1969 Introduction, 11, and the 1990 Introduction, 34).

So what about celebrating a wedding at a regular Sunday Mass? There is no general guideline that can be given since communities vary so widely in North America. In some dioceses, there is a general prohibition against celebrating weddings on Sundays at all to avoid overburdening the priests and deacons on what is usually the busiest day of the week, so the question is moot.

Having given this background, let me offer some general thoughts on this issue. In the last century, many parishes in North America had several priests, and thus had the convenience of scheduling weddings and funerals at special times rather than at the time for parish Masses. But such separate celebrations run counter to the ancient tradition of one eucharistic celebration per community per day. The custom of celebrating weddings and funerals apart from the regularly scheduled parish Masses may also need to be reevaluated in light of the availability of priests today.

Fewer active priests (some with responsibility for several parishes) may mean that Sunday weddings may not be able to be celebrated with Mass (or at all), unless a wedding is actually incorporated into the usual Sunday Mass.

Every sacramental celebration is ideally a celebration of the entire community, whether the sacrament is baptism, penance or marriage. For this reason, it is not inappropriate to celebrate a wedding when the community gathers, for instance, at a Sunday Mass, although there may be good pastoral reasons why this should not be done with any regularity.

Such a communal celebration may be more appropriate in close-knit rural communities, where the bridal couple is well known to the majority of those present at a Sunday Mass.

Although the Code of Canon Law (1248, section 1) permits the faithful to fulfill their Sunday obligation by attending any Mass (thus including a nuptial Mass), pastoral concerns would recommend that the Sunday readings not be omitted regularly (based on the principle found in the 2002 GIRM, 355, for weekday readings). Liturgical law also prohibits the use of the nuptial Mass on Sundays in Ordinary Time if this displaced a regularly scheduled parish Mass (see the *Rite of Marriage,* 1969 Introduction, 11, and the 1990 Introduction, 34). Thus, in most cases, one would use the texts and readings for the Sunday Mass with one adaptation. It is permitted to substitute one reading, as long as it is taken from the list of choices given in the *Rite of Marriage,* and it is always permitted to include a nuptial blessing after the Lord's Prayer and a special nuptial blessing at the end of Mass.

Penance

Must I (should I, how do I) use scripture when reconciling penitents individually using rite 1?

In the revision of the liturgical rites after the Second Vatican Council, an effort was made to structure all of the standard rites in a similar fashion. The typical ritual pattern, therefore, consists of an opening section that includes a greeting and perhaps an initial prayer, some sort of proclamation of the word of God, intercessory prayer, a special action or blessing and a conclusion. This pattern holds true whether the liturgy is a sacrament, such as baptism or anointing, or a simple blessing of individuals or objects (see the *Book of Blessings* [BB], Introduction, 20, 27). One important aspect of this pattern is that, as a rule, the proclamation of the word of God provides the context in which a sacrament or blessing occurs (see BB, 21).

In the 1973 revision of the rite used for celebrating the sacrament of penance, each of the three paradigms is structured in a similar way, each following the typical liturgical pattern.

In all three rites, the proclamation of God's word is included to reflect the divine initiative in the reconciliation process. The introduction of the *Rite of Penance* proclaims this truth quite eloquently: "Through the word of God the Christian receives light to recognize his or her sins and is called to conversion and to confidence in God's mercy" (17). "The sacrament of penance should begin with a hearing of God's word, because through his word God calls men and women to repentance and leads them to a true conversion of heart" (24). "Readings should be chosen which illustrate . . . the voice of God calling men and women back to conversion and ever closer conformity with Christ" (24a).

In rite 1, the rite for reconciling individual penitents, the rubric indicates that the priest may read an appropriate scripture passage or verse after the initial welcome, sign of the cross and greeting (43). (Paragraph 17 of the introduction permits the penitent to read the scripture as well.) This rubric then provides the context for the scripture by saying that the "text of Scripture . . . proclaims God's mercy and calls men and women to conversion." Because of various circumstances in which the sacrament is celebrated and various types of penitents who frequent the sacrament, the rubrics indicate that scripture is optional, one reason being that reading the scripture may have already been done as "part of the preparation for the sacrament." Nevertheless, the introduction of the *Rite of Penance,* as well as the rubrics themselves, highlights the foundational nature of scripture within the celebration of penance.

Ideally, the order given by the rite would be followed when celebrating individual reconciliation; therefore, at least one or two verses of scripture would be proclaimed after the initial greeting and before the penitent begins to confess his or her sins. For example, after the greeting, the priest might say, "In acknowledging your failures, also remember the comforting words in the gospel of Saint John: 'God so loved the world that he gave his only Son, so that everyone who believes in him might not perish but might have eternal life' (John 3:16)." Or the priest could say, "We should always remember that God reaches out to sinners, as Saint Paul tells us: 'What proves that God loves us is that Christ died for us while we were still sinners' (Romans 5:8)."

Since catechesis and training for the revised format for this sacrament was not as widespread as for other post–Vatican II rites, quite often penitents do not wait for the priest to speak any words of scripture after the greeting and before they begin confessing their sins. In such a situation, it is often possible to weave in a verse or two of scripture as a response to the penitent's confession of sins (before the priest offers counsel and assigns a penance). For example, the priest might say, "You have acknowledged your sins before God and me, his minister. Remember the comforting words in the first letter of Saint John: 'If we acknowledge our sins, then God who is faithful and just will forgive our sins and purify us from everything that is wrong' (1 John 1:9)."

Some have suggested that whenever there is a group of penitents who have gathered at a certain time for reconciliation, before the priest enters the confessional room, he might have a "mini" communal service with those present, beginning the time for individual reconciliation with a greeting, opening prayer and scripture reading. In this type of setting, there might not be the need to include another proclamation of scripture with each penitent.

Ingrained habits are hard to change. Many penitents who continue to make regular use of the individual rite of reconciliation are those who grew up with the previous rite with its set formula of "Bless me, Father, for I have sinned" and without any proclamation of the word of God. Trying to shift the expectations of such penitents will take time, energy and education, and thus will not occur overnight. In some places, pastors may need to be creative in stressing the importance of scripture. One option is to place framed quotations of appropriate scripture verses on the walls of the confessional room, easily visible to penitents. If penitents get accustomed to scripture being included somewhere during the individual celebration of reconciliation, then over time the inclusion of scripture before confessing sins may become natural.

Should I wear vestments when I hear confessions? If so, what is required? I'm not asking about communal penance services, but rather about rite 1 "in the box."

The introduction to the *Rite of Penance* does not explicitly prescribe the vestments to be worn when reconciling penitents. Since the sacrament of penance (along with the sacrament of the anointing of the sick) can be celebrated in a variety of places and circumstances, a general norm would not work. Instead, the introduction leaves the determination of which vestments are to be worn to the bishop of the diocese (14). The rite found in the 1614 Roman Ritual (Title III, Chapter I, 10) prescribed that a surplice and purple stole should be worn by the priest, but also gave some leeway by adding "as occasion and the custom of the place warrant." Prior to the reforms of Vatican II, rarely did a priest in the United States wear a surplice in a confessional "box" when hearing confessions, but the use of a purple stole alone was common practice and this continues to be the practice in many places.

The 1973 revision of the *Rite of Penance* attempted to remind all that this sacrament, like all sacraments, is a communal, liturgical celebration of the church, even though it is often celebrated in a semiprivate setting with only a minister and one penitent participating. The communal dimension is most evident when communal penance services are celebrated, but it is also present in the individual celebration of the sacrament, especially when the celebrating priest reminds the penitent in the formula of absolution that "pardon and peace" are granted "through the ministry of the Church."

Since the celebration of the sacrament of penance is a formal, liturgical rite, it is therefore appropriate that, when celebrated in a church, a priest vest as he would for other formal, noneucharistic liturgies celebrated in a church, namely with an alb and stole. This principle would hold both for communal celebrations of the sacrament as well as for individual celebrations, and the use of the same vesture by the celebrating priest may, in fact, help remind penitents of the communal and liturgical nature of the sacrament, even when celebrated "individually." The use of an alb with the stole would be particularly appropriate when the place where the individual form of the sacrament is celebrated is more of a spacious chapel or reconciliation room than an old-style "box," and the majority of penitents choose the "face to face" option rather than remaining behind a translucent grille or screen. Among other things, by wearing an alb and stole, the priest is symbolically proclaiming that the penitents and he are engaged in a public rite of prayer, not merely a private counseling session.

Of course, there are various occasions that arise where the use of the stole alone over clerical attire may be appropriate. The obvious cases would be when ministering in a hospital room, or if a person asks to receive sacramental absolution during a session focusing on counseling or spiritual direction in a rectory parlor, or even if the sacrament is celebrated in an old-style confessional without the possibility of confessing face to face. Occasionally, in certain retreat contexts, people who have been away from the sacrament for a prolonged period of time may feel more comfortable if the priest were less formally attired when they speak with him face to face.

Perhaps more than any other sacrament, the sacrament of penance is still in an ambiguous stage of renewal. People who regularly come to confess their sins often do so in an older style and using older formulas. They need to be guided to see other dimensions of a sacrament that for them has always been a very private affair. Ministers of the sacrament can assist in this ongoing renewal not only by what they say in interacting with a penitent, but also how they vest when celebrating this unique expression of God's mercy and forgiving love.

When celebrating a communal penance service, is it permitted to end the communal portion of the service before the individual confessions begin? We don't want to inconvenience our parishioners with a long wait while everyone goes to confession.

Since 1974 or so, celebrating communal forms of penance has done much to instill a sense that sin and forgiveness both have a social as well as an individual dimension. Many communal penance services follow the model in rite 2 of the 1973 *Rite of Penance,* the structure of which is similar to other sacramental celebrations: opening rite, liturgy of the word, liturgy of the sacrament, concluding rite. In the celebration of penance (following rite 2), the liturgy usually consists of a common expression of sorrow, individual confession and absolution and a communal proclamation of praise and thanksgiving after all have confessed. Often, the sharing of the sign of peace is included here as a fitting ritual gesture. The concluding rite is a simple blessing and dismissal.

Sometimes those preparing this kind of celebration feel a tension between liturgical authenticity and practical concerns, especially time constraints. By its very nature, Christian liturgy includes the assembling of the baptized, the proclamation of God's word, a sacramental action and the sending forth of the assembly. Yet when this format is attempted in the celebration of penance with individual confession and absolution, the number of people present and the time needed to minister confession and absolution sometimes means that the baptized have to stay assembled for a very long time in order to conclude the liturgy. This may be a burden for some people, especially if the liturgy is held in the evening.

Therefore, some parishes abbreviate the penance liturgy, including the opening rite, liturgy of the word, confession and absolution, but then allow each person to leave after he or she has been absolved. This service begins as a communal action but culminates in the private action of individual confession and then ends informally with individuals going off one at a time.

This compromise is less than ideal. It takes the core sacramental action—confession and absolution—out of a communal setting. Depending on how one experiences it, this format either makes the assembling of the baptized and the proclaiming of God's word a "tacked-on" preliminary, or it makes the sacramental action—confession and absolution—an afterthought. Ideally, if a communal penance service is celebrated with individual confession and absolution, the individual dimension should be integrated into the communal action. This presupposes several things.

First of all, a sufficient number of confessors should be available—perhaps one confessor for every 10 to 20 penitents. Secondly, proper catechesis should be given so that penitents understand that a communal service is not the appropriate moment for lengthy spiritual direction. Although the confessors must be pastorally sensitive, they might suggest to those penitents in need of lengthier dialogue that they come back at another time.

In addition to catechizing people properly about the differences between confessing in a communal service and confessing in the rite for individuals, the careful preparation of the worship environment may help the flow of the communal rite. It may be better not to use the confessional, and even to avoid using chairs for the confessors and penitents. Sitting may suggest that there is an unlimited time to speak. Standing has precedent in some Eastern churches, where there are no confessionals and the practice is to stand and confess, often near the icon screen. Without using the confessional or the reconciliation chapel, however, providing the option for anonymity for the penitent may prove difficult.

One adaptation that has been done in some places is to determine a time limit for individual confessions within the service, such as 15 to 20 minutes. Thus the complete celebration may take no more than an hour. When the predetermined amount of time has passed, the music ministers begin a hymn, during which the confessors and penitents reassemble for the thanksgiving and dismissal. After the dismissal, confessors can return to their locations for those who may not have had the chance to confess or for those desiring lengthier counsel.

Another option is to envision the time of individual confessions as a time for communal prayer. As individuals go to confessors, the rest of the assembly stays gathered. Psalms, scripture readings (perhaps the same ones proclaimed earlier but repeated now in smaller portions), meditative hymns, periods of reverent silence and instrumental music can be arranged in a ritual unit and repeated periodically. What some might otherwise perceive as a time of detention can thus be transformed into a prayerful vigil. This presupposes that ministers—lectors, cantors and other musicians— are prepared and rehearsed, and that the assembly has been properly catechized. People will need to know that they can prepare to make their own confessions during this "vigil time," but of equal importance, with their presence and prayer, they are supporting those who are confessing. The end of this vigil time would come when the last of the confessors returns from his station. The mood would then shift from reflective vigilance to exuberant praise with a hymn for which all would stand and sing. Finally, the liturgy would end with the sign of peace and dismissal.

The pastoral challenge is to have a parish liturgical life that allows for both individual and communal forms of penance: sensitive to the needs of the individual as well as to the needs of the community, and faithful to the public and symbolic nature of the sacrament of penance as a liturgical act.

Anointing of the Sick

Our parish celebrates the sacrament of the anointing of the sick communally several times a year at a special Mass for the sick. What are the regulations for such services?

As a result of the *Constitution on the Sacred Liturgy* (CSL) of the Second Vatican Council, the sacrament of the anointing of the sick has undergone a remarkable transformation over the last 40 years. The CSL provided a new appreciation for what, up to that time, had been called "extreme unction." In particular, it suggested that this sacrament would be better termed "the anointing of the sick" and that it was "not a sacrament for those only who are at the point of death" (73).

The introduction to the revised 1972 *Rite of Anointing and the Pastoral Care of the Sick* provides a general norm for who may receive this sacrament. It states simply that "great care and concern should be taken to see that those of the faithful whose health is seriously impaired by sickness or old age receive this sacrament" (8) and that, regarding "the seriousness of an illness," "a prudent or reasonably sure judgment, without scruple, is sufficient for deciding" (8).

The introduction also notes that the sacrament may be repeated during the same illness (if the person declines), that sick individuals may be anointed before surgery, and that elderly people who have become weakened may be anointed even if there is no serious illness present (9–11). It makes a special note that the faithful should ask for this sacrament "as soon as the right time comes" and that "they should not follow the wrongful practice of delaying the reception of the sacrament" (13).

All of these instructions point to a renewed understanding of who may receive the sacrament: It is not a sacrament only for those who are at the moment of death; rather, it is a sacrament for those whose health is "seriously impaired," but who, with God's help and medical attention, may, in fact, recover their former strength.

Even though the sacrament is not reserved for those at the moment of death, the pastoral notes in the 1983 revised English edition of the *Pastoral Care of the Sick* caution against indiscriminately anointing people, and thus watering down the meaning of "serious." It notes (99) that "the intent of the conciliar reform . . . should not be used to anoint those who are not proper subjects for the sacrament." It also notes (108) that "the practice of indiscriminately anointing numbers of people . . . simply because they are ill or have reached an advanced age is to be avoided. Only those whose health is seriously impaired by sickness or old age are proper subjects for the sacrament."

Canonist John Huels addresses in detail the question of who should be anointed in his book, *Disputed Questions in the Liturgy Today* (Chicago: LTP, 1988, pp. 91–99). In his comments on this question, Huels points out that this issue is not merely a question of following rubrics: "More is at stake here than the observance of canon law. When healthy or slightly ill persons routinely receive the anointing, its symbolic value as a special sacrament reserved for the seriously ill is jeopardized. As liturgical theologian Jennifer

Glen puts it: 'Rites that attempt to include every meaning risk losing all meaning.'"

In a sense, this sacrament is a way for a sick Christian to identify with Christ in his passion and ask for God's healing power, so evident in Christ's ministry, especially as narrated at the beginning of Mark's gospel. As the Lord himself said, it is the sick who need the doctor (see Mark 2:17). People who are seriously ill, or whose age has significantly weakened their vigor, should not hesitate to ask to receive this sacrament. On the other hand, the young and healthy, or those suffering only from a minor illness such as the common cold, risk turning the sacrament into a magician's potion or elixir if they present themselves to be anointed. This sacrament is not meant to be the spiritual "apple a day" that keeps the doctor away. It should also be emphasized that people feeling the need for emotional and spiritual healing should be encouraged, instead, to celebrate the sacrament of penance.

To help educate the local community about this sacrament, when announcing the date and time of a parish anointing liturgy, it might be good also to give some guidelines about who may appropriately ask for the sacrament. For some people, saying that those who feel "*significantly* impaired because of an illness" may make more sense than using the word "seriously." A heart condition requiring bypass surgery, cancer, HIV infection are all medical conditions that "significantly" affect the way individuals live their lives. The common cold or allergies may make people feel miserable, but usually those ailments do not "significantly" impair the way an individual functions, at least for more than a day or two. The elderly who feel the weakness of age may ask to receive the sacrament, but it probably is not helpful to suggest that "everyone over 65 can be anointed." It might also be good to emphasize that this sacrament is a means by which Christians who are conscious of being united to Christ in his suffering can ask the Father to "save [them] and raise [them] up."

The sacrament of the anointing the sick enables the church to continue the healing ministry of the Lord. Through it, the church brings the comforting touch of God's power to those who in a significant way experience the weakness and physical limitations of our frail, human condition. It is the prayer of the church that through this sacrament "the Lord in his love and mercy" may help the one suffering "by the grace of the Holy Spirit" to experience divine strength even through human weakness.

What kinds of oil may be used for the anointing of the sick? When can a priest bless the oil?

Anointing with oil had many religious uses in biblical times: coronation of a king, ordination of a priest, installation a prophet, consecration of cult objects, care of wounds, healing the sick, embalming the body. In the Mediterranean world, oil was an all-purpose medium, used in cooking, as medicine, in lamps, as a cosmetic. The oil most often used was olive. (See *And You Visited Me* by Charles Gusmer [Collegeville: The Liturgical Press (Pueblo Books), 1984], pp. 4–5.)

Oil is used in the sacrament of the sick especially for its healing and strengthening qualities, and because it signifies the presence of the Holy Spirit. Due to a more generous and frequent use of the oil of the sick, more oil is needed than in the past. The sacrament is no longer only for the dying and may be repeated when a person becomes ill again or when an illness takes a turn for the worse. The oil should also be spread generously on the sick person's forehead and hands (see *Pastoral Care of the Sick,* 107).

Paragraph 20 of the introduction to *Pastoral Care of the Sick* states that "the matter proper for the sacrament is olive oil or, according to circumstances, other oil derived from plants" (see also the 1983 Code of Canon Law [CIC], 847.1). Thus, if olive oil is not available, other plant oils (for example, corn, peanut, safflower) may be used. Church law permits any priest to bless the oil of the sick "in the case of necessity . . . only in the celebration of the sacrament" (see CIC, 999.2). In the Roman rite, following ancient tradition, the oil of the sick is normally blessed during the Chrism Mass. The norms for this sacrament respect the dignity attached to the annual episcopal blessing of this oil and thus do not permit a priest to bless oil without a "good reason." What constitutes a good reason, however, is not specified. Yet the broader tradition of the church has never insisted on the episcopal blessing of the oil of the sick as it has with the consecration of chrism. For example, the rite for anointing the sick used by Byzantine churches assumes that the presiding priest will always bless fresh oil.

The 1984 *Ceremonial of Bishops* explicitly permits a bishop to bless oil as part of the rite when he presides at a communal anointing service (654). Here, the anointing rite would parallel the baptismal rite in which fresh water is usually blessed as part of the liturgy.

Parishes should obtain enough oil of the sick during Holy Week each year to use when administering the anointing of the sick, especially during the Easter season and the following summer months. If a parish regularly celebrates communal anointing services, the oil will run out. Oil can also become rancid or otherwise deteriorate because of excessive heat or improper storage. When (or if) this happens, fresh oil will need to be blessed.

Two final comments: One, cotton has been used in oil stocks to prevent spillage when transporting holy oils, but this is not necessary in a church. There is no more danger of spilling blessed oil than of spilling consecrated wine. During a communal celebration, using appropriate glass bowls prevents the possibility of spilling the oil and makes it clear that oil—not some strange, moist, white material—is being used in the sacrament. Two, it is becoming more and more common to display the holy oil in churches. It is also common to "welcome" the oils into parish churches during Holy Week after they have been blessed by the bishop. Both customs are commendable, highlighting the importance of oils in the community's sacramental life. Too often the oils appear out of nowhere, giving the impression of using secret magical potions. Remember to keep a sense of proper proportion, however. Receiving the oils during Holy Week should never overshadow the celebration of the Lord's passion and resurrection!

How often should we celebrate the sacrament of the anointing of the sick as a communal, parish-wide celebration? We are a parish of 1,700 households, with a good number—but not a majority—of elderly people.

The *Constitution of the Sacred Liturgy* (CSL) of the Second Vatican Council reminded us that "rites which are meant to be celebrated in common . . . should as far as possible be celebrated in that way. . . . This applies with special force to the celebration of Mass . . . and to the administration of the sacraments" (27). The CSL also reminds us that the sacrament of the anointing of the sick is "not a sacrament for those only who are at the point of death" (73). As a result of these conciliar admonitions, after the revised rite for anointing the sick became available in English in 1974, there was a widespread renewal in people's understanding of the sacrament and changes in the way it was celebrated.

One significant change pertains to the recipients of this sacrament. The introduction to the 1983 *Pastoral Care of the Sick* notes that "great care and concern should be taken to see that those of the faithful whose health is seriously impaired by sickness or old age receive this sacrament" (8). It also notes that the sick may be anointed before surgery related to a serious illness (10), and that the elderly may be anointed if they have become notably weakened (11). Nevertheless, the rite still cautions against "indiscriminately anointing" people unless their health is "seriously impaired" (108).

Another change is related to the ambience in which the sacrament is celebrated. The revised rite gives directions for celebrating the sacrament of the anointing of the sick in a communal setting (mentioning, in particular, "large gatherings of a diocese, parish, or society for the sick," and "pilgrimages" [132]) and for celebrating this sacrament in a church during Mass. Since the introduction also stated that people "should not follow the wrongful practice of delaying the reception of the sacrament" (13), it became common for parishes to schedule communal celebrations, often during Mass, of the sacrament of the anointing of the sick and elderly of the parish.

In the 1970s, unlike some Eastern Catholic and Orthodox churches, which celebrate communal anointing services annually during Holy Week, Western Catholics had no tradition of such communal services. As a result, the frequency of such services varied from diocese to diocese and from parish to parish.

In some places, a communal anointing of the sick would be celebrated at a regularly scheduled weekday Mass once a month, such as a First Friday or First Saturday Mass. In other places, a specially scheduled Mass of the Sick (using the special preface and presidential prayers) would be celebrated once a year, sometimes followed by a parish reception. Parishioners living in assisted-living facilities or nursing homes near the parish church would be brought to this special celebration and priests from neighboring parishes would be invited to the liturgy to help with the laying on of hands and anointing.

Because of the basic liturgical principle that communal celebrations of the sacraments are always to be preferred to quasi-private ones, it is appropriate for every parish to schedule periodic communal celebrations of the sacrament of the anointing of the sick. The frequency of such celebrations, however, should respond to the demographics of the parish. In newer parishes in new subdivisions with younger parishioners, it might suffice to schedule a special service once a year and, if particular circumstances arise, to announce the availability of communal anointing at other times. (Some parishes have similar practices with infant baptisms in which a special Mass is scheduled once a month, but baptisms may also be scheduled during other Masses if requested.) Established parishes in older communities or near retirement facilities and convalescent hospitals may opt to schedule anointing services several times a year. One should always remember, however, that disease can strike people of every age and at any time, and a parish may have to be flexible in the scheduling of anointing liturgies.

No matter what the frequency of celebrating such an anointing service, it is very important to prepare the celebration appropriately. Music should be assigned as at any communal celebration. Well-trained readers and those familiar with distributing communion to the sick should be recruited. An appropriate number of priests should be invited—a single priest cannot be expected to anoint several hundred sick and elderly by himself. Depending on whether residents of nursing facilities have been invited, it would be good to have enough people to assist those who use wheelchairs or walkers.

Depending on the response to such a service, the parish staff might want to reflect on whether it would be appropriate to schedule such a service more or less often. If relatively few sick and elderly people come to be anointed, perhaps the interval between such services should be lengthened. If many are anointed and the service takes longer than planned, perhaps more priests need to be invited to help and services scheduled more often, rotating between geographical areas of the parish. One should also be cognizant of when such services are scheduled during the year—typically more people are sick in November and December during "flu season" than in late spring and early summer. A small attendance may mean that an anointing service was scheduled when everyone was very healthy!

One of the more notable activities of the Lord's public life was healing the sick. Healing was one of the explicit ministries entrusted to the 72 disciples (Luke 10) sent on mission. Communal services that celebrate God's healing mercy experienced through the sacrament of anointing the sick call to mind the healing power of God's love and the challenge for each of us to be instruments of healing in the midst of so much suffering in our fragile world. Thus we do well to celebrate them appropriately!

Funerals

If a family decides to cremate a relative after death, how do we convince the family to celebrate the vigil, funeral Mass and commendation first, and then cremate the body and have the committal service?

The problem with any set of options, whether it concerns something as mundane as varieties of toothpaste or something as significant as what can be done to the body after death, is that the set of options is often presented without any sort of hierarchy of preferences or without a list of pros and cons. In dealing with bereaved family members at a moment of grief, especially when death was unexpected, it may be difficult to convince them of anything. Nevertheless, it may still be appropriate to continue an ongoing education of the parish community about practices related to the funeral rites including cremation, highlighting those preferred liturgical practices recommended by the tradition of the church. Such education could take place on a regular basis by way of announcements in parish bulletins, for example, during November, the month of the faithful departed.

Until 1963, church law generally prohibited cremation. In that year, during the Second Vatican Council, Rome lifted the prohibition, yet urged that "the practice of burying the bodies of the faithful . . . by all means . . . be kept" (see the 1963 Instruction, *Piam et Constantem*). The permission for conducting funerals for those whose bodies were to be cremated was incorporated into the 1969 revised *Order of Christian Funerals* (OCF), with the note that such funerals should be conducted in a way "that clearly expresses the church's preference for the custom of burying the dead" (Introduction, 15). This preference for burying bodies rather than cremating them is still evident in the current 1983 Code of Canon Law, which states in canon 1176.3: "The church earnestly recommends that the pious custom of burying the bodies of the dead be observed; it does not, however, forbid cremation." The presupposition of the liturgical books, however, is that if cremation takes place, it would occur only *after* the funeral liturgy (either Mass or liturgy of the word) at which the body is present.

In the United States, the funeral rites may be celebrated in the presence of the cremated remains by virtue of an indult granted by Rome in 1997 at the request of the U.S. bishops. Pastoral details regarding the practice of cremation along with the rites and texts to be used are contained in "Appendix: Cremation" (or "Appendix 2") to the U.S. edition of the OCF, published in 1997 (its paragraph numbers continue that of the OCF and start with 411). This appendix, and its pastoral notes, help put the practice of cremation in context.

The church's tradition of preferring burial of the body is explicitly noted in the introduction of Appendix 2 where it states, "although cremation is now permitted by the church, it does not enjoy the same value as burial of the body. The church clearly prefers and urges that the body of the deceased be present for the funeral rites" (413). Appendix 2 also notes that funeral rites with cremated remains are subject to the approval and regulation of the diocesan bishop (426b).

There are some common practices related to the cremated ashes that are explicitly prohibited by Appendix 2. Such prohibited practices include scattering ashes on the sea or ground, or keeping the ashes in the home of a relative. Catholic practice is to treat the ashes as it treats the body—burial in a grave or entombment in a mausoleum or columbarium remains the standard ways of disposing of the earthly remains (417).

Taking these recommendations into account, the preferred order of events at a funeral of someone whose body will be cremated before burial or entombment is this: The vigil, followed by the funeral liturgy with final commendation, takes place as usual with the body present in a coffin. The usual honors are given to the body (sprinkling with holy water at the reception at the church, clothing with the white pall, incensation at the final commendation). After the final commendation (at the conclusion of the funeral liturgy), the body is taken from the church and cremation occurs (419). After the remains are ready, burial or entombment takes place with an adapted rite of committal using the appropriate texts.

There may be valid reasons, however, for choosing cremation *before* the funeral liturgy (for example, when someone dies unexpectedly in a foreign country and transporting the body back home raises financial and legal problems). In such a situation, it is permitted (with the local bishop's approval) to celebrate the funeral liturgy with the cremated remains present (427), using an appropriate choice of texts (428–429).

Sometimes people choose cremation mistakenly thinking that the funeral costs are significantly reduced. However, with a judicious choice of options (for example, an inexpensive coffin and no embalming), the cost differential can be much less than one might expect.

As with other choices found in the liturgy, not all options are of equal value. Because our faith is based on Christ's burial and resurrection, and because cremation was for many cultures an implicit denial of the afterlife, the church still prefers that the bodies of Christians be buried after death. Nevertheless, recognizing that cremation is common in many cultures and that modern society views cremation differently than in previous centuries, the church has permitted cremation while not encouraging the practice. Yet, if this option is chosen, the church still urges that the actual cremation take place only after the body of the deceased is honored with traditional gestures of reverence, especially those associated with the funeral Mass. For it is the body that was washed in baptism, anointed in confirmation and fed at the eucharist, and it is that same body that is traditionally honored with the rites associated with Christian funerals.

The *Order of Christian Funerals* prescribes a vigil service for the deceased during the "wake," but the family wants a rosary. What do we do?

The European burial customs of the sixteenth and seventeenth centuries often included burying someone's remains on the day of death or the day after death. As a result, the 1614 Roman Ritual did not envision a separate formal service before bringing the body to a church for the funeral Mass. In the section of the 1614 Roman Ritual dealing with the moment of death, the last rubric states that, until the body is moved for the funeral liturgy, "prayers should be said for the deceased by those present, whether priests or others." The section dealing with the burial rites envisioned a formal procession with the body from the home to the church. This procession was led by a priest accompanied by ministers (one of whom carried the processional cross), and was begun with the recitation of Psalm 130 ("Out of the depths I cry to you, O Lord"). During the procession, Psalm 51 ("Have mercy on me, O God") was also recited and, if necessary, additional psalms were sung. After the procession reached the church, if Mass was not to follow immediately, the Office of the Dead could be celebrated after the body was put in position before the altar.

Contemporary funeral customs, including the widespread embalming of bodies and delaying of burial to allow relatives to travel to attend the funeral rites, have led to a period of "waking" the deceased, often for several days after death, before the funeral Mass and burial. In the United States, most often such a wake occurs in a funeral home or in a parish church, but bringing the body of the deceased to the family home for a wake is not uncommon in other countries, especially in rural areas.

The absence of prescribed texts in the 1614 Roman Ritual and the inability of most people to read the Latin prayers and scriptural texts led to many families reciting the vernacular devotional prayers they knew during the period of the wake.

The revised funeral rites, published in Latin in 1969, acknowledged contemporary practices and included the recommendation of a more formal liturgical vigil before the body is brought to the church for the funeral Mass. It gave an outline of such a service with texts for a greeting, the proclamation of the word, intercessions, the Lord's Prayer and a concluding prayer.

When the English texts were revised and published as the *Order of Christian Funerals* (OCF) in 1989, the sections dealing with the vigil were expanded and the brief outline given in the earlier English version was provided with more complete rubrics and appropriate texts. The Canadian edition included several additional forms of a vigil not found in the U.S. or British editions. In addition, the OCF provides separate rites for optional use when the family first gathers around the coffin (OCF [U.S. edition], 109–118) and when the coffin is closed and prepared for transfer to the church for the funeral Mass (OCF [U.S. edition], 119–127).

When a family requests a rosary as part of the wake, sometimes this request comes from a lack of knowledge and experience of a vigil for the dead. A pastoral minister might gently suggest that the church now provides and recommends a service that includes passages from scripture that the family could select. One could also suggest that such a service might seem more welcoming to any non-Catholics present than if the rosary alone were recited. In some situations, it could be appropriate to suggest that family members pray the rosary by themselves when they first gather around the coffin, before other friends and relatives arrive for the formal wake service.

There is no reason why the rosary could not be prayed at another time, led by priest, deacon or other parish minister, or even a relative. (In fact, just as some retirees and those who do not work during the day have joined together in "resurrection choirs," perhaps leading the rosary will become another parish ministry.) The time in between the first gathering in the presence of the body and the funeral Mass need not be marked only by the official vigil, although the vigil is in fact the highpoint of that time. Other prayers and devotions can be prayed as time allows and circumstance suggests.

The family may still suggest that, since the deceased was devoted to the rosary, they would still like it to be included in the vigil. In this case, one could suggest that one or two decades, perhaps the mysteries of the resurrection and the assumption, could be included after the scripture and homily and before the intercessions and final prayer and blessing.

The vigil service during the period of the wake is a much less formal service than the funeral Mass. The Canadian edition of the OCF even recommends that family reflections and words of remembrance not be included during a funeral Mass (that is, before the final commendation as in the U.S. edition), but rather be included at the less formal vigil service. At the vigil, there is usually more time for socializing and informal remembrance before and after the actual service itself, and the ambience is often more appropriate for such remembrances than after communion at a funeral Mass. Within this sort of context, a family who insists on including at least part of the rosary during a vigil service might be encouraged to have a family member offer a brief remembrance of the deceased's devotion to the rosary and then lead those present in a recitation of a decade of this prayer.

The *Constitution on the Sacred Liturgy* of the Second Vatican Council reminds us that all devotions are secondary to official liturgical rites (13), even a devotion as beloved to many as the rosary. Such devotions have been and continue to be of great value to the faithful and should be encouraged when they respond to the spiritual needs of individuals. Pastoral ministers, however, need to continue to educate people about the surpassing value of God's word proclaimed to those gathered in Christ's name as part of an official liturgical rite and how this word can offer comfort and peace particularly in time of sorrow and loss. It is for this reason that the church recommends a vigil service that includes God's word as the most appropriate form of prayer when family and friends gather during the time of the wake.

How much ceremony is envisioned in the rite of committal? Should I wear vestments to the cemetery? Should the servers come, too? What about the musician? If so, how do we do this, practically speaking?

The original 1969 introduction to the *Order of Christian Funerals* (OCF) describes the general plan for a funeral as consisting of three "stations" (locations for prayer) with two intermediate processions (OCF, 42; Appendix, 5). The first station is the home or, more commonly in North America, a funeral parlor, followed by the procession to the church. After the funeral Mass (the second station), there is the procession to the cemetery, followed, in turn, by the third station, consisting of the committal prayers and burial.

It is not uncommon in older cities or even in contemporary rural areas for a cemetery to be located adjacent to the parish church. In such cases, the people gathered in prayer at the funeral Mass can easily walk at the end of the Mass from the church to the gravesite for the committal prayers. The OCF even provides an alternative placement for the final commendation (with the "Song of Farewell," which should always be sung [OCF (U.S. edition), 147; Appendix, 10]) for such a situation. In this case, immediately following the prayer after communion, the procession to the gravesite occurs (OCF [U.S. edition], 169) and the final commendation with the Song of Farewell, which commonly takes place in the church after communion, is integrated into the prayers at the gravesite (OCF [U.S. edition], 224). In such a case, it is most appropriate that the priest and other ministers remain vested as at Mass and lead the procession to the gravesite. If there is a choir, it is appropriate for them to lead everyone in some sort of processional hymn (OCF [U.S. edition], 41, 42, 176), perhaps even making use of the Litany of the Saints, a traditional form of prayer for processions (and easy to sing without accompaniment).

In most other circumstances, the cemetery is some distance from the church, and often the committal rite may be scheduled several hours later or even the next day, especially if the funeral Mass were held in the evening. I suggest it is always good to attempt to keep some sort of unity among the various rites related to funerals. The committal rite is, liturgically, the conclusion of the funeral Mass delayed, by necessity, because of the procession to the gravesite. It should not be seen as an entirely separate liturgical service. Just as the blessing of palms on Palm Sunday is a special form of the opening rites that precedes a formal procession, so the committal service should be seen as an elongated form of the concluding rites for the funeral Mass.

It is with this background in mind that decisions should be made regarding the committal rite. Even though, quite frequently, not everyone who is present at the funeral Mass can be present at the gravesite, it is most appropriate to link the committal rite as much as possible to the Mass that preceded it. Thus, it is very appropriate for the priest to wear an alb and stole and, if ministers who assisted at Mass are also present, it is appropriate for them to be vested as well (holding the holy water and sprinkler, if it is used). It would be possible for the priest, cantor and assisting ministers to drive to the cemetery together following the hearse or the family in order to be there with enough time to prepare themselves for the rites to follow.

After arriving at the cemetery, the priest can vest again and might even direct those present to form a procession from the hearse to the grave, symbolically continuing the procession that started at the church. The priest, ministers and cantor (or choir) would lead the mourners, reciting psalms or a litany.

If those in attendance are used to singing a cappella (or perhaps accompanied by a guitar or other instrument), it is appropriate to join in praising God through song (OCF [U.S. edition], 32, 42, 214, 223, 230, 233). Most Catholics know the Gregorian chant version of the Lord's Prayer, and many mixed groups can easily sing one verse of "Amazing grace" or "Praise God, from whom all blessings flow" from memory. Some parishes distribute funeral prayer cards with a verse of some appropriate hymn that can be sung according to some common melody (for example, "Alleluia! Alleluia! Hearts and voices heav'nward raise" [Ode to Joy]), which can also be sung a cappella at the gravesite. Some ethnic groups may have other hymns that are well known and appropriate for singing at the committal service, such as the Polish "Witaj królowo nieba" (Hail, Queen of Heaven) or "Dobry Jezu" (O Good Jesus).

If the coffin is actually lowered into the grave during the service (see OCF [U.S. edition], 209, 219), this action may be accompanied by a hymn expressing the community's faith in the resurrection.

Although funerals, especially committal services, are very emotion-filled moments, they can also be moments of great faith in a God who has given us new life through the resurrection of his Son. Any service that expresses such faith should be celebrated well, using appropriate vestments and assisting ministers (deacon, reader, servers) when available. Such faith also naturally calls for expression in song. Parishes that have become comfortable singing at Masses should, at least at larger funerals, attempt to include singing at the committal rite whenever possible. One might be surprised at how well those present can praise God in song, even in the midst of their sorrow and tears, and appreciate formal liturgical attire, even outside of a formal liturgical setting.

Is a eulogy ever permitted at a funeral?

Both the 2002 *General Instruction of the Roman Missal* (GIRM) and the introduction to the *Order of Christian Funerals* (OCF) mention that at a funeral there may be a brief homily "but never a eulogy." The Latin is *secluso tamen quovis genere laudationis funebris* (2002 GIRM, 382). Questions have been raised as to whether this is a blanket prohibition against any eulogy, or if it only means that a eulogy can never replace the homily.

Considering that various national editions of the OCF permit a friend or relative to "speak in remembrance" of the deceased either at the end of the vigil (for example, paragraph 90 in the Canadian edition or paragraph 80 in the U.S. edition) or before the final commendation (for example, paragraph 170 in the U.S. edition), it is obvious that the intent of this directive is not to prohibit any reference to the deceased during the three stations of the Christian funeral. Rather, the intent seems to be to prohibit a certain style of rhetoric during a formal address to those assembled. In particular, the rubrics prohibit someone from omitting the proclamation of the gospel message of Christ's death and resurrection—the core of any homily—and replacing it with a eulogy focusing exclusively on the achievements of the deceased.

In the way that it's used in the rubrics, the term eulogy (*laudatio funebris,* "funeral praise") seems to refer to a speech of "good words" (from the Greek *eulogia,* meaning praise, blessing or flattery) that does not refer to the gospel and, in common usage, praises the deceased, often ignoring any human weaknesses. To the extent that a speech of this form ignores the religious context in which it is being delivered, as well as the reality of human weakness and God's mercy, it is inappropriate at liturgy.

Yet this prohibition does not mean that there should be no reference to the deceased for whom we are praying. (Sample homilies for ordinations specifically have the bishop speak to those to be ordained, and rubrics in the rites of marriage and of religious profession state that the presider should adapt his words to the particular circumstances.) If the presidential prayers, including the eucharistic prayer, permit references to the deceased by name, certainly the funeral homily may also refer to the one who is now joined to Christ's resurrection!

It is an understatement to suggest that the time of death and the various funeral rites are emotionally charged moments. Family members are often dealing with grief and guilt as well as financial and legal worries all at the same time. In addition, the death may have been unexpected and traumatic. Family and friends often want to proclaim their admiration for a beloved relative or friend and may even think that it is demanded by social (or even religious) customs that someone "give a eulogy" during one of the funeral services.

In response to this, the OCF does explicitly permit someone to "speak in remembrance" at the vigil (Canadian and U.S. editions) or even before the final commendation (U.S. edition only). But this is not a required part of the liturgy and should be understood in the context of the prohibition against the homily being replaced by a eulogy.

If not monitored properly, people can experience such words of remembrance as the low point of the entire ritual action. Laypeople who are asked to deliver such statements often have little experience in public speaking, particularly at religious services, and do not realize that their "few words" can take 15 to 20 minutes to deliver. If several people have been asked to say a few words, or if the family or presider announces that "anyone else who wishes is now invited to say a few words," a simple reflection can turn a worship ceremony into a series of "one-upmanship" speeches. By their length, these reflections can relegate the proclamation of God's word and the thanksgiving for Christ's body and blood to insignificant preludes.

On the other hand, a few well-prepared statements, totaling no more than five minutes and focusing on how the deceased was an individual of faith and hope who loved and served family, friends, God and neighbor, and even with his or her imperfections was an inspiration for others, can help the grieving process immensely for those who remain in this "valley of tears."

So in general, my suggestions would be as follows:

First, avoid using the term "eulogy" for any speech during formal liturgical rites for the deceased. Depending on who speaks the words and at what point in the liturgy they occur, these addresses are a "homily," a "reflection on scripture" or faith-filled "words of remembrance."

Second, preaching, whether at the vigil or during the funeral liturgy, should be a true homily focusing on faith in God, who has given us hope through the death and resurrection of Jesus. Nevertheless, it should make reference to the reality that it is the faith of the church that the deceased has now been caught up in the reality of Christ's risen life in a way that we who are still on pilgrimage on earth must continue to hope for. Events in the life of the deceased may even provide concrete examples of how the gospel message can be lived out. If the ordained minister is related to the deceased, the homily might include enough personal reflections that additional "words of remembrance" would not be needed.

Third, if emotions, stamina and other circumstances permit, and if the homilist did not know the deceased intimately, it might also be appropriate (but not necessary) for someone to speak "in remembrance" of the deceased. This remembrance should focus on the way the deceased showed Christian virtues in life, and Christian faith and hope while approaching death. This should be done in the context of faith and should be proportionate to the rest of the rite.

It is our Christian faith that our life here on earth is a preparation for our death and that our death is a birth into eternal life. The rites of the church that are celebrated at the time of death and burial should focus on our belief that a fellow Christian has now attained the goal we all long for — union with God. Achievements on earth are ultimately insignificant when compared to this reality. Thus funeral liturgies are inappropriate moments for cataloging earthly achievements. The challenge for pastoral ministers is to respond compassionately to the desires of the bereaved family and friends, yet help them celebrate a liturgy that proclaims our common faith in our participation in Christ's resurrection.

Blessings

May lay people preside at blessings?
If so, when?

It is a long tradition that all Christians may, and at times should, utter blessings — prayers of praise and thanksgiving to God for benefits received or prayers of request for God's special care for another person. For example, we often forget that "grace before meals" is a true blessing of God and, thus, of God's gift of nourishment, whether the prayer is offered by a bishop or by a child.

Tradition also suggests that, as a rule, when those who lead the community's prayer are present (namely, bishops, priests or deacons), the office of presiding over certain blessings should be entrusted to them (see *Book of Blessings* [BB], Introduction, 18b, c, d). This practice does not deny the possibility of laypeople leading celebrations of blessings, but suggests a certain hierarchy in the choice of the one who presides when the church gathers for prayer.

Paragraph 79 of the *Constitution on the Sacred Liturgy* specifically mentions the possibility of authorized laypeople presiding at blessings (or "sacramentals," to use another term). One of the first revised liturgical rites to incorporate a prayer of blessing offered by a layperson was the 1969 *Rite of Baptism of Children*. This ritual book provides a prayer of blessing over the water in the rite used by a catechist when presiding at the baptism of children (142). Also, the practice of catechists offering blessings over catechumens is encouraged in the *Rite of Christian Initiation of Adults* (see paragraphs 95–97 in the U.S. edition).

Most of the orders contained in the revised BB specifically mention the possibility of laypeople presiding, in particular, over the blessing of sons and daughters (174). The introduction (18d) states the general principle operative:

> Other laymen and laywomen, in virtue of the universal priesthood, a dignity they possess because of their baptism and confirmation, may celebrate certain blessings, as indicated in the respective orders of blessings, by use of the rites and formularies designated for a lay minister. Such laypersons exercise this ministry in virtue of their office (for example, parents on behalf of their children) or by reason of some special liturgical ministry or in fulfillment of a particular charge in the church, as in the case in many places with religious or catechists.

The book *Catholic Household Blessings and Prayers* provides a resource for prayers and blessings celebrated in the context of the home and family. Public leadership of prayer and blessings by laypeople is an old tradition that has been overlooked in recent centuries because of an exaggerated focus on role of ordained ministers. The 1989 BB and other post–Vatican II rites provide us the opportunity to catechize our communities about various blessings — about the appropriateness of parents blessing their children, sponsors and catechists blessing catechumens and leading prayers of blessing and dedication in other situations.

Reflecting on the minister of blessing should also lead to a reflection on the meaning of blessings as well. Blessings are ways of acknowledging God's presence in various areas of creation. They are privileged ways to focus our energies on seeking God's protection on people or places, on setting material creation aside for special use, on offering thanksgiving for gifts received.

In a real sense, they can prepare us for a more fruitful reception of the sacraments. For example, blessing and thanking God for our daily bread can prepare us to celebrate the eucharist. Praying for God's blessings for someone who is ill can prepare us to celebrate the sacrament of the anointing of the sick.

Too often in the past, blessed objects have taken on a quasi-magical importance, as if they possessed more significance than, for example, the celebration of the eucharist. Blessings should always help us focus on God, on God's love seen in other people and in material creation and on our use of things to help us build up God's reign.

Can you give me some advice about whether or not to use holy water during the rites contained in the *Book of Blessings*? It seems that the old Roman Ritual always called for sprinkling an object with holy water to bless it, and the revised ritual only does so in certain rites. What gives?

The *Book of Blessings* (BB) is one of the more recent sections of the Roman Ritual to be revised after the Second Vatican Council, and thus it incorporates many of the insights about liturgical rites and symbols gained during the post-conciliar period of renewal.

One such insight, evident in the texts used for blessing and sprinkling water at the beginning of Mass, is that holy water is a reminder of the waters of baptism. Thus, its most appropriate use is with and by those who have been baptized. In other words, holy water is best used on people rather than objects. Thus we find a sprinkling with water indicated in rites pertaining to the blessing of people, as in the blessing of a family (BB, 59). When other rites in the BB call for the use of holy water (as when buildings are blessed), there often is an introductory text which links the sprinkling of water to the baptism of those assembled (see BB [U.S. edition], 87, 675, 1613).

Another insight is that it is easy for religious rites to become privatized and superstition-laden. The introduction of the BB (27) cautions against practices that could perpetuate superstitious attitudes toward blessings, such as blessing objects merely with the gesture of the sign of a cross and without any proclamation of the word or the prayer of blessing, or blessing objects by a priest alone, without anyone else present (17).

The introduction of the BB (20–23) also indicates that the major aspects of a standard rite of blessing are the public proclamation of God's word (perhaps even only a sentence in some situations), followed by a formal prayer of blessing, often with hands extended over persons or objects (26). After the prayer of blessing, the people or object should be considered "blessed" and anything else should be considered merely a supplemental or explanatory action.

Such supplemental actions can be appropriate if used in a fashion consistent with good principles of the liturgy. For example, the BB (26) states that incense is symbolic of veneration and honor for certain objects, and the rites prescribe the use of incense, after the prayer of blessing, for objects used in churches, such as the stations of the cross, the baptismal font, the presidential chair, images for public veneration or the tabernacle (see, for example, 1302).

The BB also states that water is a reminder of Christian baptism, and its use is prescribed usually when people are blessed (for example, a family [59], a family in a home [87], children [152]), or when a building that is regularly used by people is being blessed (for example, a new home [675], a seminary [697], a religious home [720]). In the case of buildings, the rubrics prescribe that people are sprinkled first and then the areas that they will inhabit. The blessing of church bells (1321) or a cemetery (1433) mentions the use both of holy water as well as of incense.

On occasion, the BB mentions some other supplemental action as appropriate after the formal prayer of blessing. For example, after blessing a scapular, the person who will receive the scapular should be formally vested with it (1499). After the blessing of a rosary, it should be used in a public recitation of the rosary (1480).

Aside from these instances, the BB mentions no use of holy water or incense in conjunction with objects of religious devotion such as statues, medals or pictures (1455). The prayer of blessing alone would be used for these items. Since such objects are for private devotional use, honoring them with incense in the way that public statues in churches are honored may be a bit too grand. The use of holy water also seems inappropriate.

By generally restricting the use of incense to public objects used or venerated in churches and the use of holy water to people and places wherein people work or live, the revised BB gives greater prominence to the formal prayer of blessing and to the baptismal nature of holy water. Indiscriminate use of liturgical symbols (including holy water) can devalue them and turn them into superstitions, rather than permit them to be seen and used in their most traditional ways. Rites of blessing are never acts of magic.

The BB, however, occasionally does seem inconsistent. For instance, the BB does allow (though does not require) the use of holy water when blessing food, drink or special objects on certain feasts of Mary or local saints (see 1796). This optional use of holy water is mentioned in the generic rite that can be used in those places that have had a tradition of special feast day blessings and want a contemporary structure for use when celebrating such a solemn rite. But, in general, the principle mentioned above (that is, that holy water is used for people and the places where they live or work) is the one that is operative in the revised BB.

One of the challenges of celebrating any liturgical rite properly is to make use of the liturgical elements appropriately. Certain elements common in the Tridentine liturgical rites are rightly omitted today, given a renewed appreciation of their meaning. Other elements, present in the Tridentine liturgical rites but often downplayed or considered secondary, are rightly highlighted today. The ongoing task of those who celebrate any liturgical rite, including the rites contained in the BB, is to celebrate these rites according to the ideal presented in the revised liturgical books. In particular, with regard to blessings, we must realize that these rites are celebrations in which we hear God's word, pray for human needs and ask God's blessing on individuals or objects. Everything should be arranged to help such a rite, even if celebrated (on rare occasions) only with a priest and one other member of the faithful present, become a true action of worship of our loving God.

Do you have any suggestions about how to handle people who bring rosaries and medals to be blessed quickly after Mass? I would like to be faithful to the *Book of Blessings,* but I dislike inconveniencing people by asking them to wait and come to the sacristy?

As with the other liturgical rites revised since the Second Vatican Council, it takes time to shift the expectations of clergy and faithful about various rites. But with education and careful implementation, experience has shown that people respond positively to a new approach to the rites. For example, people have generally accepted and even become excited about the current way to celebrate Mass, Christian initiation of adults and the anointing of the sick, three rites that have experienced major changes in the last 30 years.

The *Book of Blessings* (BB) sets as an ideal for any blessing a minimal proclamation of scripture (perhaps only one or two verses), followed by optional intercessions and concluding with a special prayer of blessing (see BB, Introduction, 20–23). The former practice of blessing an object merely by tracing the sign of the cross over the object and without any audible formula is expressly forbidden (see BB, Introduction, 27). The BB also discourages a priest from celebrating a blessing without someone else present who participates in the rite (see BB, Introduction, 17). (Thus priests should never bless an object left on the vesting table before Mass!) The minimal rite is not necessarily lengthy, but it is structured to avoid the minimalism so often associated with liturgical rites in their former versions.

One of the problems with the implementation of the BB is that the majority of the rites it contains are not those that would be regularly celebrated in most parishes in a public way, and so most people and many priests and deacons have no experience of how a typical rite should actually be celebrated. Thus, as an educational and devotional practice, perhaps parishes should consider celebrating formal blessings several times a year in conjunction with feasts or seasons and using the rites contained in the BB. The public celebration of blessings would eventually set the standard of what any rite of blessing consists. People may be less likely to feel inconvenienced if they had an expectation of what a standard rite of blessing should consist. In addition, public rites conform better to the ideal of the Second Vatican Council that public and communal rites are to be preferred to those that are private.

Parish liturgy committees might consider the following as possibilities for public blessings throughout the year:

- the blessing of families or children on the feast of the Holy Family (BB, 40, 135)

- the blessing of home candles on the feast of the Presentation (Roman Missal, February 2)

- the blessing of throats on the feast of Saint Blase (BB, [U.S. edition], 1622)

- in agricultural areas, the blessing of seeds early in the Easter season (BB [U.S. edition], 986)

- the blessing of first fruits and flowers on the feast of the Assumption (BB, 1007; see 1614 Roman Ritual, Chapter II, 17)

- the blessing of crosses for use in homes on September 14 (BB, 1442)

- the blessing of rosaries on the feast of Our Lady of the Rosary (BB, 1463)

- the blessing of food (bread and wine) on Thanksgiving Day (BB [U.S. edition], 1755).

It would be easy to incorporate such blessings into Mass, when celebrating Mass is required or appropriate, either after the homily (incorporating the prayer of blessing into the general intercessions) or, alternatively, as part of the final blessing. On weekdays, it might be possible to celebrate an independent rite of blessing immediately after Mass, inviting everyone who brought objects to be blessed to gather at some appropriate place in the church. Such formal rites should follow the structure found in the BB as much as possible, and make best use of the textual options given.

The parish liturgy committee might also consider including occasional brief explanations in the parish bulletin of the purpose of blessings (to give thanks to God who touches our lives in many ways). After reading such explanations, people may become less inclined to consider blessings as a "magical moment" by which the words of a priest alone somehow transform the object being blessed (see BB, Introduction, 27). They may, instead, see blessings more as an invocation of God's favor on those who use an object (for example, a rosary) or honor a sacred image (a cross or an icon) in their homes. Over time, some people may even come to prefer public, communal rites and parishioners may even eagerly wait for the next "blessing" day to be announced!

The ultimate blessing anyone receives is the gift of life and the gift of new life through baptism. Those gifts are renewed and refreshed through the blessing of the eucharist and of the other sacraments. Other blessings must always be seen as secondary to the sacraments, yet never be celebrated in a way to suggest they are unimportant. Priests and deacons, while responding to people in a pastoral way, should also invite individuals to a fuller celebration of these rites, so that the faithful can be challenged by God's word and in return "bless" God in prayer and praise.

Is there a blessing for a gravestone? What about a blessing for a monument commemorating someone deceased where the monument is not near the actual grave or where the body has been buried at sea?

Neither the *Order of Christian Funerals* (OCF) nor the *Book of Blessings* (BB) contains any rite specifically for blessing grave markers. Of course, it would be possible to make use of a general blessing for such an occasion, but reflection on liturgical norms may suggest that it would be preferable to avoid such a blessing.

A general liturgical principle is that the rite used should be appropriate for the person or occasion that is the focus of the rite. Thus, lesser occasions demand the use of sparser rites, and greater occasions demand fuller rites. For example, there are occasions when the liturgical books discourage celebrating a special rite during Mass. In particular, the rite used for religious profession recommends that the formal rite of accepting someone into the novitiate should *not* be celebrated during Mass. This initial rite merely marks the start of a process that reaches a highpoint with first profession and culminates in final profession, both of which are appropriately celebrated at Mass. And the BB offers wise caution about using "generic" blessings too frequently when it states (BB, 1985): "It is not fitting to turn every object or situation into an occasion for celebrating a blessing (for example, every monument erected no matter what its theme, the installation of military weapons, frivolous events)."

The absence of any form of blessing in official liturgical books for grave markers suggests to me that what is important are prayers for the deceased person rather than prayers for a physical object used to mark the grave.

Then there are questions about a blessing or rite of dedication of a monument commemorating deceased individuals in a place other than a cemetery. Such a memorial could be a plaque within the church honoring members of the armed forces who were killed in action, a statue of one of the saints in the parish garden commemorating a founding pastor or any number of other objects.

In the case of a religious object installed for general devotional purposes (an outdoor cross or statue, for example), the BB contains appropriate rites for blessing such works of art. It would be appropriate during the homily and intercessions to remember those in whose memory the religious work of art is being dedicated. In the case of a plaque of names or a similar object, one might wish to adapt the rite for visiting a cemetery and pray for those commemorated on the plaque rather than attempt any sort of blessing of the plaque itself. The merit of such a plaque is that it invites those who see it to remember those whose names are inscribed therein.

Similarly, when friends and relatives gather to dedicate a marker honoring someone buried elsewhere (for example, someone buried at sea or someone whose body is lost at sea), liturgical authenticity would suggest that the rite of committal not be used as is. Neither does it seem appropriate to bless such a monument. Rather, a memorial service could be held, modeled after a vigil for the dead or the rite for visiting a cemetery, in which the deceased is remembered by name while friends and family gather around the monument.

In these situations, as in many others, the minister should always respond compassionately to those gathered in prayer, especially at such a highly emotional time as when commemorating the dead. But good liturgical practices should always be based on solid liturgical and theological principles. Blending principles and practice is a never-ending challenge!

Devotions

I've seen different priests in our parish and in other places lead benediction in many different ways. What are the regulations for this service? Have they changed recently?

Revised norms governing exposition of the blessed sacrament and benediction were first published in 1967 in the document *Eucharisticum mysterium* (EM) (58–66), then repeated with prayers and rubrics in 1973 in *Holy Communion and Worship of the Eucharist Outside Mass* (HCWE) (82–100), and repeated again in 1984 in the *Ceremonial of Bishops* (CB) (1102–1115). Though it has been over 30 years since HCWE appeared, many priests (and even some publishers of liturgical texts and music) act as if they know nothing about any revised norms. Using old texts and rubrics violates the letter and spirit of liturgical law. In addition, since the eucharist is so central to the life of the church, anything pertaining to celebrating the eucharist or devotion toward the reserved sacrament should be done with utmost care and in the context of the entire liturgical reform since Vatican II that focuses on the celebration of the Mass.

Let me first try to put benediction (that is, "blessing" the people with a consecrated host after a period of "exposition") in some context. This rite (along with the feast of the Body and Blood of Christ [formerly Corpus Christi]) arose in Belgium only around the thirteenth century in response to controversies regarding Christ's presence in the consecrated bread and wine. Devotion to the reserved eucharist grew in the Western church in response to the Protestant Reformation and its questions about certain eucharistic practices. A rite of eucharistic benediction is generally unknown among the Eastern Christian churches (both Catholic and Orthodox), since eucharistic controversies among Christians in the East were virtually nonexistent.

The popularity of benediction before the reforms of Vatican II seems also related to a distancing of the people from participation in the Mass. During Mass, assemblies were often silent and passive, the words of the priest were not understood, few of those present went to communion and looking at the consecrated host or adoring the reserved sacrament substituted for actually receiving communion.

Official church law used to be rather reserved with respect to devotional practice surrounding the reserved sacrament. Aside from the feast of Corpus Christi, exposition of the sacrament followed by benediction was only permitted with the explicit approval of the diocesan bishop. The 1983 Code of Canon Law (CIC), in canons 941 and 942, still speaks about observing "norms," and the local bishop can issue specific norms regarding any devotional rite (see CIC, 838, section 4).

Current norms regarding the reserved eucharist place any devotions in a historical context and emphasize that any such devotion must be related to the celebration of the Mass (HCWE 82). The *Constitution on the Sacred Liturgy* reminds people that "liturgy . . . of its nature is far superior to . . . devotions" (13; see EM, 58).

For example, practices during benediction have now been harmonized with practices during Mass. In particular, reverence is shown by genuflecting on one knee (HCWE, 84; CB, 1103) instead of the former "double" genuflection, and the number of candles at benediction should be the same as at a festive Mass, that is to say, four to six candles (HCWE, 85; CB, 1104). The continued use of the seven-branch "benediction" candelabra is against the spirit of the norms.

Exposition of the eucharist does not replace and is not to compete with Mass but must be seen in relationship to it. Thus, Mass cannot be celebrated in the same area of the church where the eucharist is exposed (EM, 61; HCWE, 83). A brief exposition solely for benediction immediately after Mass is forbidden (EM, 66) or at other times (HCWE, 89). If a lengthy exposition begins after Mass, the host used should be consecrated at the Mass (EM, 60; HCWE, 94; CB, 1105).

Regarding the liturgical rite, after the priest approaches the sanctuary (while the assembly sings an appropriate song), he makes an appropriate reverence. He then removes the sacrament from the tabernacle and puts it in a monstrance or leaves it in a covered ciborium (HCWE, 93), which is usually placed on the altar. The sacrament is then incensed if a monstrance is used.

The current rubrics next prescribe "prayers, songs, and readings to direct the attention of the faithful to the worship of Christ the Lord" (EM, 62; HCWE, 95; CB, 1111) or the recitation of part of the Liturgy of the Hours (HCWE, 96), but leave the exact order up to local determination. (Roman documents first said that the rosary is not an appropriate prayer to be said publicly during such an exposition, but the curia reversed itself recently and said that the rosary should not be prohibited.) Scripture should be proclaimed from the ambo used for readings at Mass. The presider should normally be at the presidential chair during this time (see CB, 1110). A homily is explicitly mentioned along with periods of silence (EM, 62; HCWE, 95; CB, 1111), and no veil is placed before the sacrament during this time.

After the scripture, homily and silence, the priest returns to the altar and incenses the sacrament while a eucharistic hymn is sung. Then, while standing and facing the people as usual, he says (or sings) a prayer from the seven options offered (HCWE, 98). (The versicle and response, "You gave them bread . . . Having all sweetness . . ." is no longer found in the revised rite and, thus, should be considered as explicitly suppressed.)

The priest then takes the monstrance with the sacrament and, in silence, makes the sign of the cross over those assembled. After this "benediction" with the sacrament, the eucharist is immediately replaced in the tabernacle (HCWE, 100). The priest then makes the appropriate reverence in the sanctuary and returns to the sacristy while the people may sing an "acclamation" or other hymn (there is no explicit mention of the "divine praises").

A deacon may preside at this rite and give the blessing, but it is not permitted for a eucharistic minister to give the blessing, even though the diocesan bishop may permit such a minister to expose the sacrament for adoration (HCWE, 91).

The liturgical books emphasize that the "primary and original reasons for reservation of the eucharist outside of Mass is the administration of viaticum" (EM, 49; HCWE, 5). They also remind us that the "*celebration* of the eucharist is the center of the entire Christian life" (HCWE, 1), that exposition "should carefully avoid anything which might somehow obscure the principal desire of Christ in instituting the eucharist, namely, to be with us as food, medicine, and comfort" (EM, 60; HCWE, 82) and that "the celebration of the eucharistic mystery includes in a more perfect way the internal communion to which exposition seeks to lead the faithful" (HCWE, 83).

The various documents, taken together, give the impression that even though benediction is a devotion that is permitted with the consent of the diocesan bishop (HCWE, 86), it is nevertheless an optional devotion. It should be seen as distinctly secondary to the actual celebration of the eucharist, and it should be done only when "suitable numbers of the faithful" truly want it and will be present (HCWE, 86). Since this relatively recent devotion is generally unknown among Eastern Catholics, its absence in parish life cannot be seen as a lack of reverence toward the reserved eucharist. The circumstances that led to its origin and growth are far different from contemporary circumstances. Although a service that includes benediction can help foster devotion both to Christ's presence in the scripture as well as in the sacrament of the altar, a parish's first priority should be well-planned and celebrated Masses.

No liturgy or devotional rite should be celebrated unless the "spiritual good of the faithful" ultimately requires it (and not merely the personal devotion of a priest, liturgy coordinator or a particular parish group), and all decisions on the choice of liturgical texts or rites should recall this principle (see the 2002 *General Instruction of the Roman Missal*, 352). It is the maxim of the law that the "salvation of souls . . . is always the supreme law of the Church" (CIC, 1752). If benediction is celebrated in conformity with liturgical law and spirit, it can provide an opportunity for those in attendance to offer praise to Christ, who nourishes us through his word and feeds us with his sacrament. But this rite is only one of several means in which a deeper eucharistic devotion can be fostered. The challenge of our day and age is, while respecting the devotion of our ancestors, to see whether there are other ways of praising our risen Lord, who feeds, heals, forgives and saves us, that better respond to our contemporary spirituality, pieties and needs, and are also in the best liturgical traditions of our church.

Do you have any suggestions about how we might incorporate into daily Mass devotions to Our Mother of Perpetual Help, Saint Anthony and the Divine Mercy? These are important to various groups in the parish who now just rush through them before Mass.

The *Constitution on the Sacred Liturgy* (CSL) refers to "popular devotions" and recommends them, as long as they conform to the church's norms. Nevertheless, the CSL cautions that such devotions should "harmonize" with the liturgical seasons, "accord" with the liturgy and "lead" people to the "liturgy." The reason for these cautions is that "the liturgy by its very nature is far superior to any" devotion (see CSL, 13). In such texts, "liturgy" refers to the official prayer of the church, that is, the body of Christ united with Christ its head, as it praises and worships the Father, guided by the Spirit (see CSL, 7). The liturgy is not exclusively identified with the eucharist or with the other sacraments, since other rites, in particular the Liturgy of the Hours, are also considered public liturgical celebrations. The CSL, however, does suggest that not every prayer service should be considered to be "liturgy" in the strict sense of this term.

Writing about 10 years after the Second Vatican Council, Paul VI referred to section 13 of the CSL when writing about devotion to Mary in his 1974 apostolic exhortation, *Marialis Cultus.* In reference to "novenas or similar practices of piety," the pope warned about the inclination to insert devotional prayers into a Mass. He suggested that one should never make the Mass "an occasion, as it were, for devotional practices." Finally, he, in a sense, made the admonitions of the CSL more explicit when he stated that "exercises of piety should be harmonized with the liturgy, not merged into it" (*Marialis Cultus,* 31).

In December of 2001, the Congregation for Divine Worship and the Discipline of the Sacraments issued its *Directory on Popular Piety and the Liturgy*. It clearly states, "The objective difference between pious exercises and devotional practices should always be clear in expressions of worship. Hence, the formulae proper to pious exercises should not be commingled with the liturgical actions. Acts of devotion and piety are external to the celebration of the holy eucharist and of the other sacraments" (13).

In some places, there exist longstanding traditions of popular devotions associated with times of the year (such as novenas related to feasts of Mary or another saint), or even days of the week (such as Fridays in honor of the Sacred Heart). Such devotions may even be connected with a work of art within the church or a shrine (such as a chapel in honor of Our Lady of Guadalupe). Unfortunately, some of these devotions use texts and a format that predate the Second Vatican Council. The ongoing challenge of any parish community is to channel the spiritual energies and piety of the community so that its members may be spiritually built up by devotions to various saints, to Mary or to Christ under a specific title, yet realize that any such devotion is necessarily secondary to the primary sources of God's grace—the celebration of the eucharist and other liturgies.

Faithful to the directives cited above, local liturgical planners, when dealing with well-liked parish devotions, should carefully avoid any sort of merging of such devotions and non-liturgical prayers into the Mass. Instead, planners should consider our contemporary understanding of the nature of the various liturgical rites, and then see how local devotions can be harmonized with authentic liturgical practices. Sometimes this may mean that, at most, reference is made to the devotion in the homily or in the general intercessions. If the devotion is christocentric, it might be possible to harmonize some of the devotional prayers with the contemporary liturgy and use them outside of Mass, for example, within a celebration of eucharistic exposition.

In many other cases, it would probably be best to keep liturgical rites distinct from devotional prayers and practices. Thus, if a devotion involved honoring an image of Mary or other saint, with the recitation of special prayers directed to Mary or to the saint, this devotion would best be scheduled as a separate service held apart from Mass. It should also be arranged in a format that includes the proclamation of scripture and intercessory prayer, elements not always found in rites published before the Second Vatican Council. One example of a devotion that has been appropriately revised is the blessing of throats found in the U.S. version of the *Book of Blessings* (1622–1655). In this case, sample intercessions ask for healing for all the sick, and the prayer of blessing is carefully worded to emphasize that God is being asked to protect the faithful Christian from diseases of the throat, but that this request is made through the intercession of Saint Blase. When scheduling any such devotions, one should ideally have some length of time between the devotion and Mass, taking guidance from the norms regarding benediction, which forbid eucharistic exposition merely for the sake of benediction immediately after Mass.

Certainly it would be improper and misleading to merge devotional prayers with liturgical texts in such a way that, for example, a "blessing" is reworded so that the text implies that a saint is blessing the assembly rather than God. It is probably also improper to "bless" the assembly with an image of Mary or some other saint. (Liturgical tradition permits blessing others with the hand, with the book of the gospels at a Mass celebrated by a bishop or with the eucharist at benediction). It may even be a questionable practice to imitate the gesture of laying on of hands during the anointing of the sick, or to associate a gesture of reverence, such as a kiss, with divine favor. Although in Eastern Churches, it is common for members of the assembly to venerate icons with a kiss, and in the Roman rite, the ordained ministers venerate the altar and book of the gospels with a kiss, and the entire assembly honors the cross similarly on Good Friday, we should make sure that these gestures never degenerate into superstitious-like practices.

The Second Vatican Council's teaching that "the liturgy by its very nature is far superior to any" devotion and Pope Paul's statement that "exercises of piety should be harmonized with the liturgy, not merged into it" are both maxims that we need to keep in mind as we respond to the spiritual needs and devotional tastes of members of parish communities. The church has never restricted the prayer life of Christians to liturgical rites alone. Yet non-liturgical prayers must always be seen in the context of the liturgy, which ultimately is the prayer of Christ, the head with his body, to his Father.

Since the new Roman Missal says that the Second Sunday of Easter is now also to be known as "Divine Mercy Sunday," are we supposed to be adding to the liturgy of this day, such as the Divine Mercy chaplet?

Biblical and liturgical texts regularly refer to God's mercy, but a focused devotion to the mercy of God under the title of "Divine Mercy" gained momentum due to the efforts and writings of Sister Faustina Kowalska, who died in 1938. Sister Faustina lived for many years in Krakow, the city where John Paul II was bishop before his election as pope. (He canonized Sister Faustina in 2000.) The devotion of Divine Mercy was popularized in Krakow and is associated with prayers (the "chaplet of mercy") and an image of Christ with rays of light emanating from his heart and with the words "Jesus, I trust in you" inscribed on the image.

The Second Vatican Council, although commending popular devotions, was also very cautious about them, stipulating that they should "harmonize with the liturgical seasons, [and] accord with the sacred liturgy . . . since the liturgy by its very nature far surpasses any of them" (see the *Constitution on the Sacred Liturgy* [CSL], 13). Hence, there has been a great reluctance by Vatican officials to compromise the renewed emphasis on the great feasts and seasons, particularly Sundays and the Lent and Easter seasons. This is in keeping with the CSL, which noted in addressing the revision of the liturgical year that "other celebrations, unless they be truly of overriding importance, must not have precedence over Sunday" (106).

This was reiterated recently in the Congregation for Divine Worship and the Discipline of the Sacraments' 2001 *Directory on Popular Piety and the Liturgy*. It states, "The faithful should be made conscious of the preeminence of the liturgy over any other possible form of legitimate Christian prayer. While sacramental actions are *necessary* to life in Christ, the various forms of popular piety are properly *optional*" (11). For many people, the devotion to Divine Mercy is one way of expressing the ministry of reconciliation expressed in a special way in the gospel of John's account of Easter evening when the Lord tells the apostles, "Whose sins you shall forgive, they are forgiven." This gospel is used on the Second Sunday of Easter and Sister Faustina sought to have this day celebrated as a "Feast of Divine Mercy." The devotion to Divine Mercy (and to Sister Faustina) grew in popularity in Poland, and in 1995 the pope granted the request of the bishops of Poland to observe the Sunday after Easter as "Divine Mercy Sunday."

In May of 2000, the year in which Sister Faustina was canonized, the observance of "Divine Mercy Sunday" was extended to the entire Roman rite. A decree was issued from the Congregation for Divine Worship and the Discipline of the Sacraments announcing that, in the Roman Missal, the title of the Second Sunday of Easter will be followed by the additional designation "or Divine Mercy Sunday." In addition, the same decree noted that the liturgical texts currently in the Roman Missal and in the Liturgy of the Hours are "always to be used for the liturgical celebration of this Sunday." Careful reading of the decree reveals that the official text retains the formal designation of this Sunday as "The Second Sunday of Easter." In other words, we continue to celebrate the Lord's resurrection on this octave day of Easter and the current liturgical texts are not to be changed. But this day has been given a secondary designation, that of "Divine Mercy Sunday," bringing out one of the themes of the gospel, that of forgiveness of sins.

It is important to note the balance in the Vatican decree. The title of "Divine Mercy Sunday" is an added designation and should not overshadow the fact that this day is a continuation of the celebration of Easter. To put this in context, Paul VI, in his 1973 apostolic exhortation on devotion to Mary (*Marialis Cultus*), reminded people that popular devotions should be harmonized with the liturgy rather than merged into it (31). And the Congregation's 2001 directory clearly states, "The formulae proper to pious exercises should not be commingled with the liturgical actions. . . . Thus precedence must always be given to Sunday, solemnities, and to the liturgical seasons and days" (13). So the decree on Divine Mercy Sunday is an attempt to harmonize a devotion to Christ into the liturgical season without doing damage to the fundamental importance of Easter.

To answer the question directly, in accordance with the Vatican decree, no special texts are to be added to the texts already found in the Roman Missal for the Second Sunday of Easter. There is also no need to obtain the image of Divine Mercy or to enthrone such an image, if one is in use in the parish. This Sunday is primarily a continuation of the celebration of Christ's resurrection and of the biblical apparition that occurred a week after the resurrection with the dialogue between Jesus and Saint Thomas. To emphasize that this is still a celebration of Easter, the liturgy should end with the Easter dismissal (including the double Alleluia, as prescribed in the Roman Missal).

One of the criticisms of the Lord was that he showed mercy too frequently, especially to those whom the society of his day often overlooked: the sick, the lepers, the tax collectors, the sinners. Honoring God's mercy, as expressed in the life of Christ, is thus very appropriate. In line with conciliar decrees, however, any devotion must always harmonize with our liturgical celebration of the fundamental mysteries of our faith: the death and resurrection of Christ.

Architecture and Furnishings

Is there new legislation that recommends placing the tabernacle in the center of the sanctuary?

A simple answer to this question is "no."

The revised *General Instruction of the Roman Missal* (GIRM) that appeared in 2000 and (with additional revisions) with the third edition of the Roman Missal in 2002 includes an updated version of the norms that had appeared in the former GIRM regarding the location of the tabernacle. The 1975 GIRM (276) encouraged the use of a blessed sacrament chapel. But if this were not possible, it allowed reserving the sacrament in some other place that was "worthy and properly adorned." The 2002 GIRM keeps the substance of this in paragraph 314 (by specifying a section of the church that is "truly prominent, distinguished, readily vivsible, beautifully decorated and suitable for prayer") and then expands on the foundational rule in paragraph 315 by making four points:

1. The tabernacle should not be on the altar at which Mass is celebrated.

2. The placement of the tabernacle is regulated by the diocesan bishop.

3. The tabernacle may be in the sanctuary, away from the altar used for the eucharist.

4. The tabernacle may be in a special chapel (which, according to the footnote, is the preferable location).

Whereas the previous text made no mention of the common practice of situating a tabernacle in the sanctuary where the altar used for Mass is located, the 2002 GIRM now explicitly notes this as an option, harmonizing the regulations in the Roman Missal with what is common practice in many parts of the world.

One should note that in the subsection that speaks about locating the tabernacle in a "chapel suitable for private adoration and prayer of the faithful," there is a footnote to paragraph 53 of the 1967 document *Eucharisticum mysterium.* This paragraph states, "It is therefore recommended that, as far as possible, the tabernacle be placed in a chapel distinct from the middle or central part of the church."

This 1967 instruction was referenced several times by the former GIRM, and the 2002 GIRM has included additional recommendations taken from this instruction, although not always explicitly referring to it via a footnote (see 2002 GIRM 19, 114, 160). Thus the principles contained in the instruction should still be considered to be relevant and not superseded.

The 2002 GIRM also includes a recommendation (not found explicitly in the former GIRM) that the tabernacle not be on the altar on which Mass is celebrated (315). This is in line with what is found in the *Ceremonial of Bishops* (CB), where the rules state that if a bishop celebrates at an altar where there happens to be a tabernacle, the blessed sacrament should be removed (49).

It is noteworthy that the 2002 GIRM adds a clarifying regulation (274) about when one should genuflect before the tabernacle. If the tabernacle is in the sanctuary, the ministers genuflect to it when they come to or leave the altar area (at the beginning and end of Mass), but not during Mass itself. Thus the tabernacle, if it is in the sanctuary, is to be "reverently ignored" during the celebration of Mass. Some may consider this to be irreverent, but the fundamental supposition of the GIRM is that the tabernacle is a place for reservation of the eucharist apart from Mass and plays no role during the celebration of Mass itself. The 2002 GIRM makes this point even stronger than the earlier version by an addition found in paragraph 85, which refers to the people receiving communion from what had been consecrated at that Mass. The 2002 GIRM adds the words "as the priest himself is bound to do," emphasizing that both priest and people should receive from what is consecrated rather than from what is in the tabernacle.

One should not argue that because the "tabernacle in the sanctuary" option is the first one given in the 2002 GIRM, that location is the preferred option. Such an argument ignores the fact that the footnote associated with the "tabernacle in a separate chapel" option says this location is to be "recommended." It also ignores other places in the GIRM where the second option is the liturgically preferred option, but the first option is one corresponding to recent historical practices such as communion under one kind versus communion under both kinds (2002 GIRM, 161) or cleansing at the altar versus at the credence table (2002 GIRM, 163). Note that paragraph 279 of the GIRM explicitly recommends cleansing at the credence table, even though this is the second option listed in paragraph 163!

There may be practical reasons for keeping the tabernacle in the sanctuary in older churches, either on the old "high altar" or in another place. The 2002 GIRM now explicitly permits this option. There are good liturgical and pastoral reasons for placing the tabernacle in a separate blessed sacrament chapel in new churches, a chapel easily accessible for prayer if the body of the church is in use for special services (for example, weddings or funerals). The 2002 GIRM explicitly permits this option and other documents from the Holy See recommend this option as well (see CB, 49). The 2002 GIRM explicitly prohibits placing the tabernacle on the altar used for Mass, but it leaves ultimate pastoral judgments in the hands of the local bishop, who moderates the liturgical life of the diocese.

What should we do with holy oils left over from the previous year?

One of the practical items that was not addressed in the revised liturgical books relates to the disposal of old holy oils when, each year at the end of Lent, the parish receives a fresh supply after the chrism Mass. In recent years, churches have publicly displayed the holy oils, and doing so in larger and larger quantities. Thus it is no longer a simple matter of burning a couple of small oil-soaked pieces of cotton.

Lacking any explicit guidance in the revised liturgical books, we might turn to the 1614 Roman Ritual for advice and direction. There, the preliminary rubrics before the rite of infant baptism include an explicit note that the old oils are to be burned in church (Title II, Chapter 1, 48). One translation of the text adds "in the sanctuary light" in parentheses, even though these words do not appear in the Latin.

The sanctuary light seems to have been the traditional place for disposing of all old blessed oil, even those oils blessed in honor of certain saints. It was a long custom (though not common in the United States) that the sanctuary light be an olive oil lamp. Such an oil lamp is the first option mentioned in the 1917 Code of Canon Law (1271) and repeated in the 1973 segment of the revised Roman Ritual, "Holy Communion and Worship of the Eucharist outside Mass" (11) and in the 2002 *General Instruction of the Roman Missal*. (The 1983 Code of Canon Law [940] does not explicitly determine the nature of the lamp, leaving that to the liturgical books.) The use of a beeswax candle or other wax candle for the sanctuary light is a more recent practice. Since the sanctuary light would always be burning, it would be the logical place to dispose of the holy oils in the seventeenth century when the ritual was published, and so an explicit mention was not deemed necessary. In those churches in which this more traditional lamp burns near the tabernacle, it would be an easy task to renew the oil it contains with the holy oils from the previous year.

Those churches that find themselves with a large quantity of holy oils at the end of Lent might give serious thought to using the oil in some sort of oil lamp to be burnt in the church at least for the duration of the Easter season. Or the old holy oils might also be burnt in the new fire at the Easter Vigil. For very small quantities of oil, one can pour the oil onto a quantity of cotton and burn the cotton, burying the ashes. It is not a good idea to dispose of the oils in the sacrarium or in a hole dug in the earth.

Ideally, there would not be so much oil left that this would be of much concern, but even the best of plans cannot foresee everything. If there is a significant amount of oil left over, one should modify plans as to how much oil is procured from the cathedral for the next year.

The disposal of old oils is just one instance that calls for reverence for objects used in liturgy, especially those that are central to sacramental rites as are the holy oils. Our tradition has held in reverence those items used in divine worship, even after they have outlived their usefulness. They are never merely thrown out with profane rubbish but are disposed of either through burning or in some other reverential manner. The manner in which they are disposed should reflect their former holy use and the community's caring attitude toward all aspects and objects connected with its worship.

How much holy oil is appropriate for public display in our church's ambry? I would like to have a good quantity of oil to express the lavishness of God's Spirit and the full richness of the symbol, but the cathedral has limited the amount it dispenses!

Reserving the holy oils in glass decanters and in a transparent ambry is a relatively recent phenomenon. For centuries, the oils were usually kept in a locked opaque cabinet, often recessed into the wall of the sanctuary. The current Code of Canon Law (847) merely states that a pastor should obtain the oils from his bishop each year and store them appropriately. Some might consider that keeping the oils in a cabinet in the sacristy does not honor them appropriately, considering their importance in the sacraments. But perhaps newer practices deserve a bit more reflection before becoming set-in-stone customs.

The use of three different oils in the sacraments is universal in all ritual families of the church. The oil of the sick is essential to the sacrament of the sick, sacred chrism is central to confirmation and it is used during ordination as well. Though not considered essential to baptism, the oil of catechumens is used during the catechumenate for adults and prior to the baptism of infants. Knowledge of the history and different traditions pertaining to the oils can provide a context for practices relating to their reverent reservation and display.

In many Eastern traditions, a priest blesses the oil of catechumens and the oil of the sick on each occasion it is needed. Thus the only oil ever reserved in many Eastern churches is the sacred chrism, which is sometimes merely placed next to the tabernacle. Additionally, in some Eastern traditions, the chrism is only consecrated once every several years and is much more highly scented than in the West, as if it were a precious perfume that is diluted by oil, rather than an oil that is lightly scented.

Since, in the Western tradition, fresh oil is blessed each year before the Easter Triduum, it seems inappropriate to keep large quantities of oils solely for display, amounts that could not reasonably be used during the course of one year. In addition, since the rubrics permit the priest to bless the oil of catechumens (for pastoral *benefit*) as part of the rites of the catechumenate or to bless the oil of the sick (for pastoral *need*), there should be no worry about exhausting the supply of these two blessed oils. In fact, too large an amount of oil could become rancid and unusable if it is not kept properly.

The intention behind displaying large amounts of all three of the oils is a good one. Liturgy works by means of signs perceptible to the senses. Displaying beautiful vessels large enough for a church building is a way of proclaiming the importance of what the church does with different oils in various sacraments and liturgical rites. But since the oils are intended to be *used* and not displayed, the danger exists of turning them into a kind of prop. The blessing of oil before anointing catechumens or before the anointing the sick, done by the presider, is a way of drawing attention to the sign of oil in conjunction with its ritual use. So perhaps it might be a stronger sign to display only the sacred chrism — the only oil that cannot be blessed by a priest. The chrism links the local community to its bishop; reverently displayed, it gives witness that this local church is part of a larger one.

The next issue is where the ambry used for reserving the oils should be located. The chrism and the oil of catechumens are both linked to baptism, so it might be appropriate (depending on the design of the place) to reserve them near the baptismal font. But there is no such immediate link between the oil of the sick and baptism. In a sense, then, it is somewhat incongruous to store the oil of the sick near the font merely because it an oil and the other two blessed oils may be stored there.

It is also debatable whether it is ideal for the ambry to be transparent. Liturgical tradition (and canon law) considers transparent tabernacles for the eucharistic bread to be inappropriate:

There is a difference between reservation and exposition. In many ways, the reservation of the oils is not that different. If the ambry is not transparent, the question of large amounts for public display becomes moot!

Since a priest cannot bless chrism, the question of how much should be reserved in a church arises. If one is influenced by the Eastern tradition, in which chrism is considered a precious perfume, one might be hesitant to reserve too large a quantity. Even a small quantity of fine perfume can cost around a hundred dollars. Perhaps in such a situation, a small quantity does not indicate symbolic minimalism but rather the preciousness of the symbol.

But the minute quantities that were (and often still are) used when a priest pressed his thumb into a cotton-filled oil stock bespeaks of a minimal approach to sacramental symbolism. Such practices should be discouraged in our age of renewed appreciation of the fullness of the sacramental symbols. So whenever the oils are used in churches in liturgical rites, I recommend using glass containers without any cotton, and encourage bishops, priests and deacons to use enough oil that the recipient can sense the presence of oil on their heads and hands.

Yet even a more generous use of oil does not demand vast quantities during the course of the year. It is a rare parish that does not have oils from previous years that need to be disposed of each Easter!

Because the practice of publicly displaying the holy oils is such a recent phenomenon, we should be cautious about decisions made regarding this display. My concluding advice is very tentative, therefore. I would advise that enough oil be obtained so that it is visible in a worthy container when used in church for liturgical rites. In larger parishes in which numerous confirmations and baptisms occur, it would be good to get a sufficient amount of chrism so that the chrism need not be applied miserly when it is meant to symbolize the abundance of the Spirit. On the other hand, one should never obtain so much oil (a liter, for example) that the majority of it would need to be discarded the next year! To have a substantial quantity (say, half a liter) of oil left over, which was obtained only for public display, would seem to be as much of an abuse as to consecrate so much wine at Mass as to have several liters left over!

Other details regarding which oils to display, where to display them and the form and materials used for the ambry may be left up to local creativity, always mindful of the purpose of the oils and solid liturgical principles and customs.

I am the pastor of (and only priest in) two small, quite distinct parishes. I have been able to schedule separate liturgies on Holy Thursday and Good Friday, but for Holy Saturday it's impossible. The two communities have been able to compromise on the location of a single Easter Vigil, but a question has been raised about what sort of "blessing" of the Easter candle should take place for the parish that did not host the Vigil.

Besides the use of festive vestments, one of the key visible characteristics of the Easter season in the Roman rite has been the presence of an Easter candle burning brightly near the ambo. The solemn blessing of fire and lighting of the candle, the procession with the candle into a darkened church and the joyous Exsultet sung in praise of the radiance of the candle representing the light of Christ in a darkened world are key elements of the first part of the Easter Vigil.

When one carefully examines the texts of the Vigil, however, one notices that the candle itself is never actually blessed—the bonfire is. Inscribing the candle using the words "Christ yesterday and today," putting grains of incense in the candle using another formula and lighting the candle with the words "May the light of Christ, rising in glory, dispel the darkness of our hearts and minds" are all secondary rites that underline the dignity of the Easter candle. They do not constitute any sort of "blessing."

Since the Easter candle is such a key symbol for Western Catholics during the season of Easter and is used at baptisms and funerals throughout the year, it is important that every church or chapel regularly used for worship, especially those in which baptisms and funerals are celebrated, should have an Easter candle, and that this candle should be burning brightly at Masses during the Easter season.

If the Easter Vigil is not celebrated in a church or chapel, there is no reason why an Easter candle cannot be placed next to the ambo and lit without any special ceremony when the altar candles are lit for Masses on Easter Sunday morning. Especially for smaller chapels, such as in houses of religious or in Catholic hospitals, this is usually the best solution. It is the lit candle that is symbolic of the risen Lord. In a sense, the Easter Vigil merely marks the first time that this candle is lit during the 50 days of celebration.

In some situations (or for some communities), it may be desirable to acknowledge that the Easter Vigil is a common celebration of several communities and that the "light of Christ" that is celebrated at this Easter celebration is meant to be taken back into our separate homes and localities. Among some Eastern Christians, it is a common practice to take home some of the "light" of the vigil by keeping individual candles lit as people return home from the Easter Vigil. Some authors have even suggested that it would make a greater impact if the Easter candle were kept burning continuously throughout the season of Easter, or at least appear to do so by making sure that the candle is never extinguished publicly and always lit before the assembly arrives. Others have suggested that the tabernacle lamp be lit from the Easter candle at the Vigil and that, during the Easter season, the Easter candle be lit from this perpetual flame and all other candles always be lit from the Easter candle!

The circumstances in North America are such that many churches do not host a celebration of the Easter Vigil. The reasons for this vary. In some places, separate parishes have been administratively combined, but each of the original parish churches is still kept in use with a reduced schedule. In other places, a single priest is in charge of more than one parish and must travel between churches each weekend and holy day. In other places, a parish sponsors a mission church several miles away from the central church.

If some effort has been made to bring communities that are accustomed to worshiping in separate churches together for a common Easter Vigil, it might be helpful to acknowledge the presence of these different communities. This could be done at the conclusion of the Vigil in a simple fashion. For example, before the solemn blessing, a representative of each of the other communities brings to the sanctuary an Easter candle destined to be used in the particular community's church. Then the presider can light each Easter candle from the one that has been burning brightly throughout the liturgy. Representatives of the other communities could carry these additional candles as part of the procession, extinguish them in the sacristy and then bring them to the other churches before the first Mass on Easter Sunday morning.

Although this simple rite is in no way a "blessing" of the other Easter candles, it may help in a public fashion to connect the Easter candle of a local church with a celebration of the Easter Vigil, even if the local church was unable to host the Vigil for one reason or another. At the same time, it does not compromise the unity of the light of Christ that is symbolized through the presence of a single Easter candle throughout the rest of the Vigil. You certainly do not want more than one Easter candle burning during the Vigil!

The Roman liturgy is noted for its stark simplicity. Thus, one should not add or create rites needlessly. On the other hand, the Roman Missal assumes that each parish church will be celebrating its own Easter Vigil, a situation that does not always occur. In such cases, one makes do as best as possible, realizing that the Easter candle finds its ultimate meaning not in any special blessing, but as a radiant symbol of the risen Christ, who is forever the light of the world.

Is it required by canon law or liturgical law that a parish church building have the stations of the cross? Is permission from the Franciscans still required to erect the stations?

Originating around the fourteenth century, the "stations of the cross" is a relatively recent devotion in the history of the Western church, and its introduction into church buildings even more recent. The devotion originated in an attempt to offer a visual reminder of the Lord's last day on earth to those who could not make a pilgrimage to the Holy Land and, at the same time, provide them with the opportunity to benefit from the indulgences associated with an actual pilgrimage to the holy city of Jerusalem.

Since the Franciscans have been the official custodians of shrines in the Holy Land for centuries, they were instrumental in spreading the devotion of the stations of the cross in Catholic communities throughout Europe. As a result, officially blessing or "erecting" the stations was reserved to Franciscan priests before the liturgical changes resulting from the Second Vatican Council.

The physical stations commemorating the events of Christ's passion were originally set up *outside* of church buildings to give individuals taking part in the devotion a sense of movement, as if they were actually retracing the Lord's footsteps in Jerusalem. This is the format still found, for example, at some retreat centers or monasteries and, in some sense, is the ideal since it gives the participants a sense of an actual journey. It was not until 1731 that the number of stations was fixed at 14 by Clement XII. Still later, in 1742, Benedict XIV exhorted pastors to have stations erected in all churches, but it was never required that every church or chapel have a set of stations.

The first post–Vatican II liturgical instruction, *Inter Oecumenici*, eliminated the practice of "reserved" blessings in general (77), but it still reserved the blessing of stations to the local bishop or to someone delegated by him. In 1984 the *Book of Blessings* (BB) was promulgated as a successor to the section of the Roman Ritual that contained blessings. This book contains an order for the blessing of stations of the cross (BB [U.S. edition], 1400–1416) and designates the rector of the church in which the stations are being erected as the celebrant of the rite. (It does permit the rector to depute someone else, however.) It also notes that if stations of the cross have been installed in a new church prior to its dedication or blessing, a distinct celebration to bless the stations is not required.

In recent years, the traditional version of this devotion has been questioned on several grounds, the primary ones being (1) the non-scriptural origin of several of the stations (for example, Christ meeting Veronica) and (2) the division of the unity of the paschal mystery by a lack of reference to Christ's resurrection in this devotion, something the official liturgy mentions even on Good Friday. Thus, some places have officially introduced, with the Vatican's approval, a different set of "titles" for the stations. For example, one version approved for Taiwan in 1986 begins with the Last Supper as the first station and includes the resurrection as the fourteenth station. The papal celebration of the stations of the cross in the Coliseum on Good Friday has, since 1991, used variations of the traditional version. To include a fuller expression of the paschal mystery in this devotion, some communities that have the traditional stations installed in older churches have merely modified the traditional devotion by concluding the "passion stations" with the resurrection as the fifteenth station, which is often prayed before the altar or tabernacle.

At some new churches, the stations have been erected outside the nave of the church, sometimes in an outside garden area surrounding a church, following the earliest tradition of this devotion, and using only crosses, rather than any accompanying images (which are, in fact, optional). In other new churches, the stations are installed seasonally (during Lent, for example), when the devotion is prayed communally. (But that doesn't serve the needs of those who pray the devotion individually throughout the year.)

Since the stations of the cross is not an official liturgical rite, but mainly a supplemental devotion, no community needs to have stations inside or associated with a church or chapel. No specific mention is made of the stations in the *General Instruction of the Roman Missal* or in the *Rite of Dedication of a Church*. There is no official text that must be used in praying this devotion either; the only requirements are mental prayer and movement from station to station during the devotion. This devotion is very dear to the hearts of many Catholics, especially during Lent, and the attachment of the faithful to devotions that can highlight the Lord's invitation to "follow me" and "carry your cross" (Luke 9:23, 14:27, 23:26) should be dealt with appropriately and sensitively. The tradition of enshrining sacred images for the devotion of the faithful — in the right number and order — should be maintained. We should always keep in mind the devotions that are important in our community, and how the architecture and art can best serve those devotions outside of the liturgy, while flowing from it and leading back to it.

When the parish in which I work remodeled its church in the 1970s, the American and Vatican flags were removed. In light of the tragic events of September 11, 2001, some have suggested that at least the national flag should be displayed prominently. Any thoughts?

In the *Order of Christian Funerals,* the pastoral notes state that "national flags . . . have no place in the funeral liturgy" (U.S. edition, 38), and thus they "are to be removed from the coffin at the entrance of the church" (132). This rubric refers to the custom of using the national flag as a funeral pall over the coffin of a soldier or veteran, but the underlying principle on which the rubric is based can also be applied more generally.

National flags are meant to separate peoples. They are meant to inspire allegiance to civil authorities. They are reminders of "the things that are Caesar's." The church building is a place to unite peoples—a place to remind every person that all authority comes from God, a place to render to God "the things that are God's." In the United States, with its tradition of separation of church and state, the Catholic church has only recently, and still somewhat reluctantly, bridged the gap between the two by composing Mass texts for civil holidays, such as July 4 or Thanksgiving.

Unfortunately, such restraint in bridging the gap between church and state was not always practiced in the past. Thus, particularly due to a real (though often unexpressed) desire to prove that American Catholics could be loyal to the U.S. Constitution and at the same time loyal to the pope, civil flags (U.S. and Vatican) were commonly displayed in prominent places in churches.

In 1978 the U.S. Bishops' Committee on the Liturgy discreetly suggested that national symbols (such as flags) have no place as *permanent* parts of the ambience of worship (*Environment and*

Art in Catholic Worship, 101). The committee reiterated this in 2001. Such symbols may, however, be appropriate at a worship service associated with a special national holiday, such as Independence Day, for example. The 2000 document of the U.S. bishops' conference, *Built of Living Stones,* does not speak about flags or other national symbols directly, but merely focuses on what the liturgical books prescribe is needed for worship and addresses a few other items related to popular devotion, such as the stations of the cross or sacred images.

At this time in history, very few question the civil loyalty of American Catholics. Catholic civil servants are no longer regularly asked whether they would listen to the pope rather than obey the law of the land. Most U.S. citizens do not take the anti-Catholic propaganda of groups such as the Ku Klux Klan seriously. Thus, there is no need to affirm our corporate allegiance to the U.S. Constitution by prominently and regularly displaying the national flag in our sanctuaries.

On the contrary, there are significant reasons why a national flag should *not* be permanently displayed in a church—a place in which everyone (not merely U.S. citizens) is welcomed, a place in which a gospel message that often challenges the values of the country should be heard. In many parishes, there are numerous individuals who are not American citizens, or who are opposed to government policy on certain issues (abortion being a chief example). The mere presence of the American flag can send mixed messages (to some, it might suggest that the church condones all actions of the state) and be a source of division (various members in the assembly may be violently opposed to certain government policies while others support them).

Traditionally, a church was considered to be almost extraterritorial—hence the custom of "sanctuary" in a church for those seeking refuge from civil authorities. Such a tradition is compromised with the prominent presence of civil symbols.

Such are the general principles, but sometimes special circumstances suggest that particular accommodations may be appropriate. The United States, and perhaps most of the world, was left with a certain numbness in response to the horrendous events of September 11, 2001. Many perceived these terrorist events to be an act of war on the United States and felt that proudly displaying the national flag, even in churches, would be an appropriate act of patriotism along with the singing of national hymns such as "America, the Beautiful."

Such an extraordinary event cannot be ignored and elicits emotions in each person that often need to be expressed visibly. For many people, the most appropriate way to express that emotion of solidarity with the victims, the relief workers, the military and others was to display the national flag. In this context, the *temporary* presence of the flag in a church might be appropriate. Ideally, it would be placed outside the sanctuary, perhaps as part of a memorial shrine. It would also be appropriate to acknowledge that citizens of many other nations also perished in the tragedy. We must always remember, however, that any church is the place where "enemies begin to speak to one another" (Eucharistic Prayer for Reconciliation II). For this reason, such a use of the flag should be temporary.

A flag is a symbol, just like the crucifix or the tabernacle light, and we cannot limit the multiple feelings such a symbol may evoke in those who see it. Because of a heightened contemporary sensitivity to symbol in liturgy, and because of the negative connotations of alliances between civil and religious authorities, it is probably best to avoid the permanent presence of national or papal flags in churches.

If you enjoyed the answers to these questions, look for *Q&A: The Mass* by Dennis C. Smolarski, SJ. Available from Liturgy Training Publications, it is an informative book of frequently asked questions and insightful answers about celebrating the Mass. Visit our website at *www.ltp.org* or call 1-800-933-1800.

And receive a regular dose of Dennis Smolarski's pastoral wisdom by reading his Q&A column in *Rite* magazine, published six times a year, every other month. To subscribe, go to our website at *www.ltp.org,* send a message to *orders@ltp.org* or call 1-800-933-4213. The magazine also gives you an invitation and e-mail address by which you can submit *your* questions about any aspect of liturgy. A single subscription in the United States costs $18.00 a year, and foreign and group rates are also available.